Collins

11+

English

Quick Practice Tests
Ages 10-11
Book 2

Shelley Welsh

Contents

ACKNOWLEDGEMENTS

The author and publisher are grateful to the copyright holders for permission to use quoted materials and images.

pp.4–5, extract from *Giant* by Nicola Skinner, reprinted by permission of HarperCollins*Publishers* Ltd, © Nicola Skinner, 2023

pp.14–15, extract from *Shark* by Paul de Gelder, reprinted by permission of HarperCollins*Publishers* Ltd, © Paul de Gelder, 2023

pp.24–25, extract from *Dimanche Diller* by Henrietta Branford, reprinted by permission of HarperCollins*Publishers* Ltd, © Henrietta Branford, 1996

pp.34–35, extract from 'The Highwayman' by Alfred Noyes, reprinted by permission of the Society of Authors Literary Estates. The Society of Authors is the Literary Representative of the Estate of Alfred Noyes.

pp.44–45, extract from *Last Hours on Everest* by Graham Hoyland, reprinted by permission of HarperCollins*Publishers* Ltd, © Graham Hoyland, 2013

pp.54–55, 'St John: Turtle Soup' by James Draven, reprinted by permission, © James Draven

pp.64–65, extract from *Finding Bear* by Hannah Gold, reprinted by permission of HarperCollins*Publishers* Ltd, © Hannah Gold, 2023

Every effort has been made to trace copyright holders and obtain their permission for the use of copyright material. The author and publisher will gladly receive information enabling them to rectify any error or omission in subsequent editions. All facts are correct at time of going to press.

Published by Collins

An imprint of HarperCollins*Publishers* Limited

1 London Bridge Street

London SE1 9GF

HarperCollins*Publishers*

Macken House, 39/40 Mayor Street Upper,

Dublin 1, D01 C9W8, Ireland

ISBN: 978-0-00-870118-5

First published 2025

10 9 8 7 6 5 4 3 2 1

© HarperCollins*Publishers* Limited 2025

British Library Cataloguing in Publication Data.

A CIP record of this book is available from the British Library.

Author: Shelley Welsh

Publisher: Clare Souza

Project Manager: Richard Toms

Editorial: Charlotte Christensen

Cover Design: Sarah Duxbury

Text and Page Design: Ian Wrigley

Layout and Artwork: Q2A Media

Production: Bethany Brohm

Printed in India by Multivista Global Pvt. Ltd.

MIX
Paper | Supporting responsible forestry
FSC™ C007454
FSC www.fsc.org

This book contains FSC™ certified paper and other controlled sources to ensure responsible forest management.

For more information visit: www.harpercollins.co.uk/green

About this book

Familiarisation with 11+ test-style questions is a critical step in preparing your child for the 11+ selection tests. This book gives children lots of opportunities to test themselves in short, manageable bursts, helping to build confidence and improve the chance of test success.

It contains 29 tests designed to develop key English skills.

- Each test is designed to be completed within a short amount of time. Frequent, short bursts of revision are found to be more productive than lengthier sessions.

- GL Assessment tests can be quite time-pressured so these practice tests will help your child become accustomed to this style of questioning.

- We recommend your child uses a pencil to complete the tests, so that they can rub out the answers and try again at a later date if necessary.

- Children will need a pencil and a rubber to complete the tests as well as some spare paper for rough working. They will also need to be able to see a clock/watch and should have a quiet place in which to do the tests.

- Answers to every question are provided at the back of the book, with explanations given where appropriate.

- After completing the tests, children should revisit their weaker areas and attempt to improve their scores and timings.

For more information about 11+ preparation and other practice resources available from Collins, go to our website at:

collins.co.uk/11plus

Comprehension

Read the text below and answer the questions that follow. In each question, circle the letter next to the correct answer.

EXAMPLE

Nicolas's eyes were the size of dinner plates when he saw the number of presents under the Christmas tree.

Which adjective best describes how Nicolas was feeling?

A   Furious

(B)   Excited

C   Afraid

D   Jealous

E   Frightened

The following is an extract from *Giant* by Nicola Skinner

THE FIRST TIME Minnie Wadlow broke a rule from the *How to Manage Your Giant – a Giant Ownership Manual for Children* she blamed the heatwave. The second time, she blamed her giant. By the third, fourth and fifth times, she had run out of excuses.

It all started in the lagoon, a vast body of water so dark it was like swimming in ink. It was in
5   the west, only a short stroll from Minnie's home, Quake Quarter.

Minnie loved that lagoon. Unlike the toxic sludge of the Five Bridges river, whose length spanned the island, or the wreckage-infested ocean that surrounded it, the lagoon itself was clean, safe and not as likely to poison or kill you. Its attractions included a rusty waterslide, a kiosk for ice creams, and hordes of huge, feathered screecher birds, who were either screaming
10   grumpily at each other about when they were going to eat next, or feeding lumps of meat to their young and screaming happily about that.

Despite the screams of the screecher birds, the lagoon was Minnie's second favourite place. (The bakery in Quake Quarter was the first, and if you were lucky enough to try their almond and honey pastries, you'd know why.)

15   On this particular day, Scarred Island was exceptionally hot. The sun showed no mercy to the island, or its inhabitants, that day. Metal seats left outside for too long caused huge blisters on bare legs. Flies droned in and out of windows, stunning themselves on the glass. Babies grew flushed and feverish. And the caged jackals down at the meat factory, whose cries could normally be heard all over the island, were too hot to do anything but whimper.

20   Usually on such a day the lagoon would have been crowded with Minnie's classmates whizzing down the waterslide, telling their giants to fetch them an ice cream, or throwing rocks at the

screechers for fun. But Florin Athelstan was having his ceremony that day, with Sandborn, his giant. Florin's family was the most powerful on the island. No expense had been spared on the feast. So the islanders were excited. They wanted to look smart. They were too busy getting
25 ready. Despite the heat and the sun, the lagoon's dark waters lay almost empty.

There was only one child swimming in its shallows: Minnie Wadlow, a small feeble girl who'd slither about in your arms like a slippery trout if you tried to hug her. This was on account of the greasy sun cream she was always slathered in, even when it rained. Her tangled, unwashed brown hair grew down to her waist in a ratty, knotty clump, and she had a nose that some
30 people privately thought was a bit too big for her face. When it was school photo time, Minnie Wadlow was always asked to stand at the back.

While she swam in the lagoon, sending plumes of oily sunblock into the water, her classmates from Quake School were otherwise engaged, walking into beauty salons and barber shops so they could get primped and preened for Florin's ceremony. But Minnie had nothing like that
35 planned at all. Her parents didn't believe in any of that stuff on ceremony days, or on any other day for that matter. Quite the opposite, in fact. If anything, they practically *encouraged* her to look scruffy and dirty.

'You don't need to brush your hair too much, or wash your face, or do any of that nonsense,' they'd say. 'Just be yourself Minnie. Pick that lovely distinctive nose of yours whenever you
40 want, and don't *ever* feel you need to use too much soap, darling.'

Minnie's neighbours all agreed that Minnie Wadlow was as free as a screecher bird, as smelly as a jackal cage, and as grubby as the river path. They never said that to her face though, because they had manners. They also said awful things about her parents, but that doesn't concern us now. (Oh all right. If you *must* know, they said her mother was an ageing beauty
45 who contributed very little to the moral backbone of the place, and her father's earthquake-prevention designs were next to useless. They said terrible things about the state of the Wadlow house too, which we shall not repeat here because we're not gossips.)

So greasy, grubby, little Minnie Wadlow had the lagoon all to herself! For the first time *ever*! All that water, all that *space*, all to herself, made her giddy.

---

(1) How does the lagoon differ from the Five Bridges river and the ocean?

   A   It is as dark as ink.

   B   It is clean and safe.

   C   It is a vast body of water.

   D   It is in the west.

   E   It is infested with wreckage.

(2) Where is Minnie's favourite place?

   A   The lagoon

   B   Scarred Island

   C   Five Bridges river

   D   Quake Quarter bakery

   E   Her home in Quake Quarter

Questions continue on next page

③ 'The sun showed no mercy to the island, or its inhabitants, that day.' (lines 15–16)

What does this sentence tell you about the day Minnie goes to Scarred Island?

A The metal seats had been left in the sun too long.

B The lagoon water had evaporated thanks to the sun.

C The sun made the flies drone in and out of windows.

D The islanders had to leave to escape the sun.

E No one could escape the high temperatures.

④ Why are the lagoon's dark waters 'almost empty'? (line 25)

A Everyone was too busy eating ice cream.

B People were throwing rocks at the screechers.

C The islanders were getting ready for a feast.

D No one wanted to swim with Minnie.

E The lagoon was full of oily sunblock.

⑤ Why didn't Minnie get 'primped and preened' for the ceremony? (line 34)

A Her parents didn't believe in it.

B She liked to look scruffy and dirty.

C She didn't like beauty salons.

D She was allergic to soap.

E She had no money for the beauty salon.

⑥ Why was Minnie asked to stand at the back for school photos?

A Because she was the tallest in the class

B So that she could pick her distinctive nose

C To escape the glare of the fierce sun

D On account of her dirty hair and large nose

E Because she was incredibly shy

⑦ Why didn't Minnie's neighbours criticise her scruffiness to her face?

A They preferred to tell her parents.

B They were too polite.

C They weren't gossips.

D She was too smelly.

E They had no moral backbone.

8 '...the toxic sludge of the Five Bridges river...' (line 6)

Which word is closest in meaning to 'toxic'?

A   Dirty

B   Dark

C   Slippery

D   Poisonous

E   Thick

9 'Minnie's neighbours all agreed that Minnie Wadlow was as free as a screecher bird, as smelly as a jackal cage, and as grubby as the river path.' (lines 41–42)

Which literary technique is used here?

A   Metaphor

B   Alliteration

C   Personification

D   Simile

E   Rhetoric

10 'And the caged jackals down at the meat factory, whose cries could normally be heard all over the island, were too hot to do anything but whimper.' (lines 18–19)

Which of these words is a verb?

A   heard

B   cries

C   caged

D   over

E   normally

Spelling

In each question, circle the letter below the group of words containing a spelling mistake.

If there is no mistake, circle the letter N.

EXAMPLE

Jack used a cleer varnish to protect and strengthen the boat's teak deck.

(A)　　　　B　　　　C　　　　D　　　　　N

---

(1) The hikers marvelled at the thunder and lightening from the safety of the cave.

　　A　　　　B　　　　C　　　　D　　　　N

(2) Our teacher said there were insufficeint funds for the new computer equipment.

　　A　　　　B　　　　C　　　　D　　　　N

(3) The soaring tempratures have resulted in a surge of people buying air conditioning.

　　A　　　　B　　　　C　　　　D　　　　N

(4) By the time he returned from walking his dog in the fields, Raj was thuroughly soaked.

　　A　　　　B　　　　C　　　　D　　　　N

(5) My cousin exagerates so frequently that her friends are starting to question what she says.

　　A　　　　B　　　　C　　　　D　　　　N

(6) We could tell that the sailing yahct was in severe difficulties from the way it was listing.

A B C D N

(7) The wounded soldier lapsed in and out of consciousness for several days

A B C

but is now recovering well.

D N

(8) Our hotel last year was quite disappointing so Mum is now looking for

A B C

alternative acommodation.

D N

(9) Confronted by the head teacher, the mischievious boy was unable to explain

A B C

his poor behaviour.

D N

(10) My aunty was disappointed that she only scored fourty out of fifty

A B C

in her final mathematics exam.

D N

(11) Becky, who has lived in a variety of different countries, can speak three langauges fluently.

A B C D N

(12) The opening of the new liesure complex has been indefinitely postponed for financial reasons.

A B C D N

Score: .... / 12

9

In each question, circle the letter below the group of words containing a punctuation mistake.

If there is no mistake, circle the letter **N**.

EXAMPLE

Brogan's little brother, who's called Joe scratched his best friend's new bike in the park today.

    A   **B**   C   D   N

---

(1) Tanya, my so called best friend, hasn't asked me to her forthcoming birthday party.

    A   B   C   D   N

(2) We've been waiting for ages for our amazon delivery of three books and a jigsaw.

    A   B   C   D   N

(3) Without giving it a second thought Bill dived into the canal to rescue the dog's owner.

    A   B   C   D   N

(4) "Please see me in my office at precisely three o'clock", said Viv's boss, Mr Manners.

    A   B   C   D   N

(5) There's been another sighting of a UFO but the source seemingly isn't very credible.

    A   B   C   D   N

6 The Natural History museum in London exhibits a vast range of natural history specimens.
    A   B   C   D   **N**

7 I'd have thought that Javier would've expressed more excitement
    A   B   C

when he saw Mums new car.
    D   **N**

8 The fire bell – clearly a hoax was typical of Lin but still, we all
    A   B   C

had to file into the playground.
    D   **N**

9 "Are you coming to the cinema with us later?' asked Jan. "We're meeting for pizza first."
    A   B   C   D   **N**

10 I've been walking in the Lake District for many years now but I'd
    A   B   C

say Crag Hills my favourite.
    D   **N**

11 "Didn't you say you'd finished you're homework?" Ged asked. "So why are you still writing?"
    A   B   C   D   **N**

12 Dad has decided to recover the old armchair in a velvet fabric.
    A   B   C   D   **N**

Score: .... / 12

Test	# Sentence Completion
4	You have 6 minutes to complete this test. You have 12 questions to complete within the time given.

In each question, circle the letter below the word or group of words that most accurately completes each sentence.

EXAMPLE

We decided to | **parting** | **taken** | **participation** | **participate** | **part take** | in the Spelling Bee.
           A   B   C   Ⓓ   E

---

① "Can you help me with my homework?" Jan | **reported** | **implied** | **asked** |
                                        A   B   C

     | **offered** | **exclaimed** | .
        D   E

② Bea stayed with her aunt in | **hers** | **there** | **her** | **those** | **these** | house by the sea.
                                A   B   C   D   E

③ Tanya held on to the rope | **tense** | **tighten** | **tight** | **tights** | **tightly** | as Tee pulled her up.
                          A   B   C   D   E

④ We | **ought to** | **would've** | **may be** | **should be** | **should have** | invite Will to the party.
        A   B   C   D   E

⑤ Before my run, I spent ten minutes | **exercises** | **exercising** | **exercised** |
                                        A   B   C

     | **exercise** | **had exercised** | .
        D   E

⑥ Harry | **fill** | **filled** | **full** | **fills** | **filed** | up his water bottle and went out to play.
          A   B   C   D   E

(7) **For** **Since** **As** **Although** **When** the teacher had said, it was a challenging test.
    A   B   C   D   E

(8) Mum and Dad invited **they're** **their** **there** **them** **that** friends to dinner.
                      A   B   C   D   E

(9) "Come quickly!" said Ely **breathless** **breathfully** **breathe** **breathing** **breathlessly**.
                     A   B   C   D   E

"The dog's run off!"

(10) The new library wasn't quite what we **have expected** **were expected** **had expected**
                                  A   B   C

expect **expectation**.
  D   E

(11) "It **can** **would** **might be** **ought to be** **shall be** a good idea to bring a
     A   B   C   D   E

waterproof," said Dad.

(12) With no time to **loses** **loss** **lose** **loose** **leave**, we ran down the busy platform
                A   B   C   D   E

to the waiting train.

Score: .... / 12

Test	# Comprehension
5	You have 10 minutes to complete this test. You have 10 questions to complete within the time given.

Read the text below and answer the questions that follow. In each question, circle the letter next to the correct answer.

EXAMPLE

Nicolas's eyes were the size of dinner plates when he saw the number of presents under the Christmas tree.

Which adjective best describes how Nicolas was feeling?

A   Furious

Ⓑ   Excited

C   Afraid

D   Jealous

E   Frightened

The following is an extract from the introduction to *Shark* by Paul de Gelder

Like billions of other people around the world, to hear the word 'shark!' once filled me with terror, and why not? Think of those huge, gaping jaws filled with razor-sharp teeth. I bet that everyone reading this book has at some point worried about becoming a meal for one of these animals.

5   Where does that fear come from? Headlines like 'Man-eating sea monster stalks the coastline killing surfer' certainly don't help. As a young boy growing up in Australia, I spent a lot of time in the water, and movies like *Jaws* had me so scared of sharks that I'd even think about them in the swimming pools that I used to compete in (this could also be James Bond's fault, as tanks full of ravenous sharks are used by the bad guys in four – yes, *four* – of the franchise's films).

10   Of course, some explanation for our fear of sharks lies in the power of our imagination. I loved movies like *Jaws* and James Bond as a kid because they were stories well told, and while not every one of us will write a blockbuster, we are all the writer and director of the movies in our mind, and many of the stories that we create for ourselves are horrors. There's probably a good reason for that – perhaps the overactive imagination of our ancestors helped save them

15   from ending up in a sabre-tooth tiger's belly – but too often in life we let the fear that we have created override fact and truth. Are some people attacked by sharks? Yes, and we'll talk about some of them, but the truth is that far more people drown in their own bathtubs than are attacked by sharks. So why is it that so many of us are afraid to dip our toe in the ocean, but we have no worries about getting into a hot bath with a glass of wine?

20 Australia is a country that has a reputation for deadly and dangerous creatures. A lot of people I meet around the world tell me that they'd love to visit my home country, but they're too scared of the wildlife. Believe it or not, most Australians don't ever encounter these creatures in their entire lifetime. Zoos, aquariums and reptile parks are very popular attractions with visitors and the locals in Australia. From behind thick glass, or looking down from above,
25 anxious spectators can get a look at massive crocodiles, deadly snakes and venomous spiders.

In aquariums, you can watch the rhythmic swimming of a grey nurse shark. They may have beady yellow eyes, but grey nurse sharks have only ever bitten humans when provoked, and they've never killed one, so they're hardly the stuff of nightmares.

As for the apex predators that sit atop of the ocean's food chains, such as tiger sharks,
30 makos and of course, the great whites, people have tried to contain these beautiful creatures in captivity, but every attempt has failed, and the animal has perished. These marvels of the underwater realm are wild and free, and the majority of humans will never see one in their lifetime – not in person, and definitely not as they're being eaten by one.

That didn't stop me being afraid of them as a kid. I'd go spearfishing with my grandfather and
35 boogie-boarding on huge swells with my brother. I knew there were sharks out there, and I constantly thought they'd want to take a bite out of me, but some things worried me more than being eaten alive, like impressing my dad. My pride was stronger than my fear, but I didn't ever conquer my terror – I simply pushed it to one side, rather than forcing myself to confront what scared me.

40 That was my way of dealing with most things as a kid and a young adult. I was a bit of a wayward youth, but something that I always had was a love of nature and a desire to see more of the world. To put it short, I wanted an adventure.

---

1 Which two reasons does Paul give for having a fear of sharks?

    A   Growing up in Australia and swimming competitions

    B   Newspaper headlines and films about sharks

    C   Films about sharks and growing up in Australia

    D   Newspaper headlines and his overactive imagination

    E   Swimming competitions and bathtub drownings

2 What is a surprising statistic about sharks attacking people?

    A   More people die from drinking wine.

    B   Our ancestors ended up in the bellies of sabre-tooth tigers.

    C   People can see sharks in aquariums.

    D   More people drown in their own bathtubs.

    E   Australia has a reputation for dangerous creatures.

Questions continue on next page

③ What was the result of trying to keep 'apex predators' in captivity?

    A   They attacked each other.

    B   They were popular attractions.

    C   They became wild and free.

    D   They attacked the staff.

    E   The animals died.

④ What does Paul mean by 'My pride was stronger than my fear, ...' (line 37)?

    A   He'd rather impress his dad than confront his fear.

    B   He faced his terror but didn't conquer it.

    C   He forced himself to confront his fear.

    D   He was proud of his boogie-boarding skills.

    E   He was proud of spearfishing with his grandfather.

⑤ What kind of questions are these in the third paragraph?

'Are some people attacked by sharks?' and '...why is it that so many of us are afraid to dip our toe in the ocean, but we have no worries about getting into a hot bath with a glass of wine?'

    A   Imperative

    B   Informative

    C   Emphatic

    D   Rhetorical

    E   Exclamatory

⑥ Why might our ancestors' overactive imaginations have helped save them from being eaten by sabre-tooth tigers?

    A   They let their fear override fact and truth.

    B   They imagined that sabre-tooth tigers were safe.

    C   Their fear of attack would have made them cautious.

    D   They imagined drinking wine in a hot bath was more dangerous.

    E   They hadn't seen scary movies like *Jaws*.

⑦ What kind of adjectives are 'razor-sharp' (line 2) and 'man-eating' (line 5)?

    A   Superlative

    B   Compound

    C   Concrete

    D   Coordinate

    E   Comparative

8 Which word is closest in meaning to 'realm' (line 32)?

A   Kingdom

B   Ocean

C   Surface

D   Wildlife

E   Deep

9 Why should visitors to Australia **not** be scared of its wildlife?

A   Any dangerous creatures are kept in captivity.

B   Aquariums are popular attractions with visitors.

C   There are many antidotes now if you get poisoned.

D   Any deadly creatures have perished.

E   Most Australians do not come across deadly creatures.

10 '...tanks full of ravenous sharks are used by the bad guys in four – yes, *four* – of the franchise's films).' (lines 8–9)

Why has Paul repeated '*four*', writing it in parenthesis and using italics?

A   To remind us

B   To show how many

C   For emphasis

D   In case we misread it

E   Italics look interesting.

Score: .... / 10

Spelling

You have 6 minutes to complete this test.

You have 12 questions to complete within the time given.

In each question, circle the letter below the group of words containing a spelling mistake.

If there is no mistake, circle the letter **N**.

EXAMPLE

Jack used a cleer varnish to protect and strengthen the boat's teak deck.

(A)　　B　　C　　D　　**N**

---

① Our tetchy nieghbour has actually agreed to accept delivery of a parcel when we are away.

A　　B　　C　　D　　**N**

---

② We have a partner school in Namibia with whom we corespond via emails and letters.

A　　B　　C　　D　　**N**

---

③ The new Italian restaurant in our village serves excelent pizza, pasta and dessert.

A　　B　　C　　D　　**N**

---

④ When I first saw Ben, he seemed quite familiar but it appears he has an identical twin brother.

A　　B　　C　　D　　**N**

---

⑤ Mia assisted the health and safety commitee in identifying potential dangers in the playground.

A　　B　　C　　D　　**N**

---

⑥ Mr Rogers brought a bouquet of flowers to his grandmother's grave in the church cemetry.

A　　B　　C　　D　　**N**

(7) Hussein hastily took the oportunity to overtake the lead runner as they neared the finish line.

A   B   C   D   N

(8) The tragic sight of the long-suffering bear in captivity continued to occuppy Bert's thoughts.

A   B   C   D   N

(9) Ffion was unable to participate in the hurdles race due to a pulled mussel in her calf.

A   B   C   D   N

(10) Dad attatched a photo of us celebrating Mum's birthday to the email he sent to his cousin.

A   B   C   D   N

(11) After assuring her that the film wasn't scary, we pursuaded Li to accompany us to the cinema.

A   B   C   D   N

(12) We read poems with ryhming couplets today and now our teacher wants us to write our own.

A   B   C   D   N

Score: .... / 12

19

In each question, circle the letter below the group of words containing a punctuation mistake.

If there is no mistake, circle the letter **N**.

EXAMPLE

Brogan's little brother, who's called Joe scratched his best friend's new bike in the park today.

    A   (B)   C   D   N

---

1 "There'd better be a good reason for not completing your homework again," said Mrs Kahn

    A   B   C   D   N

2 If you don't' keep stirring the sauce, it'll stick to the bottom of the pan and you'll burn it.

    A   B   C   D   N

3 The park keeper's wheelbarrow's have been thrown in the pond by some unruly teenagers.

    A   B   C   D   N

4 Margot can't wait to visit her cousins in Australia it's just the long flight she isn't relishing.

    A   B   C   D   N

5 My best friend's house is up for sale it's over-priced in my opinion.

    A   B   C   D   N

6 The dog, full of excitement, leaped up when Jodie came home, wagging it's tail enthusiastically.

    A   B   C   D   N

(7) I'm always struggling to remember that nine times eight is seventy two,

      A   **B**   **C**

yet I know nine times twelve.

      D   **N**

(8) Theo and Vic aren't keen on the new Harry potter book but they've agreed

      A   **B**   **C**

they'll watch the film.

      D   **N**

(9) "Please help me hang out the washing", Mum said. "There are some pegs in that basket."

      A   **B**   **C**   **D**   **N**

(10) I've no idea whether we'll be able to go to the beach as the weather's so unpredictable.

      A   **B**   **C**   **D**   **N**

(11) Our neighbours have the most up to date flat-screen TV, which dominates their kitchen.

      A   **B**   **C**   **D**   **N**

(12) After a huge meal, which included bread and butter, we were served

      A   **B**   **C**

ice cream, cake, and biscuits.

      D   **N**

Score: .... / 12

Sentence Completion

You have 6 minutes to complete this test.

You have 12 questions to complete within the time given.

In each question, circle the letter below the word or group of words that most accurately completes each sentence.

EXAMPLE

We decided to | **parting** | **taken** | **participation** | **participate** | **part take** | in the Spelling Bee.
A   B   C   (D)   E

(1) Fred | **always** | **almost** | **often** | **sometimes** | **frequently** | cried when he realised he'd
   A   B   C   D   E

broken Mum's favourite vase.

(2) We've been | **waiving** | **waited** | **waiting** | **weighing** | **weighting** | for the train for
   A   B   C   D   E

about an hour.

(3) | **Finally** | **Tomorrow** | **Now** | **Next week** | **Thoroughly** | , we reached our destination:
   A   B   C   D   E

a cottage by the sea!

(4) Connie completed the jigsaw puzzle in record | **minutes** | **moments** | **seconds** |
                                          A   B   C

| **finish** | **time** | .
  D   E

5. Large | **digits** | **group** | **crowd** | **numbers** | **teams** | of people gathered to glimpse

           A   B   C   D   E

the celebrity.

6. Martha was | **mistake** | **mistook** | **mistaken** | **mistaking** | **mistakes** | about the

             A   B   C   D   E

amount of sugar required in the recipe.

7. We | **would of** | **would have** | **wouldn't** | **would** | **will have** | taken the short cut if we'd

           A   B   C   D   E

known the traffic was so bad.

8. Chris | **does** | **didn't** | **done** | **doing** | **did** | her homework at her friend's house yesterday.

           A   B   C   D   E

9. "Please can I | **borrow** | **leaned** | **lend** | **loan** | **burrow** | your umbrella?" asked Paula.

                 A   B   C   D   E

10. The trainer said Tessa's dog was the | **clevererest** | **cleverly** | **cleverest** |

                                         A   B   C

| **cleverer** | **clever** | of them all.

       D   E

11. "It's not my | **vault** | **volt** | **fault** | **fate** | **failed** | that the bath overflowed," said Kai.

                A   B   C   D   E

12. We gasped as a | **herd** | **group** | **school** | **fleet** | **pride** | of lions approached the safari jeep.

                  A   B   C   D   E

Score: .... / 12

23

Comprehension

Read the text below and answer the questions that follow. In each question, circle the letter next to the correct answer.

EXAMPLE

Nicolas's eyes were the size of dinner plates when he saw the number of presents under the Christmas tree.

Which adjective best describes how Nicolas was feeling?

A Furious

B Excited

C Afraid

D Jealous

E Frightened

The following is an extract from *Dimanche Diller* by Henrietta Branford

Dimanche was three years old when Polly Pugh arrived at Hilton Hall, the house her parents had lived in before they were lost at sea when she was just a baby. And let me tell you right now, this is not one of those stories in which the missing parents turn up at the end. You must just take it from me that every now and then fate deals someone a cruel blow. It dealt

5 Dimanche Diller several, and the first and the worst of them was the loss of her mother and father. This is how it happened.

Sailing in their yacht *Hippolytus* among the rocky islands of the Cyclades, the Dillers were set upon by one of those storms that seem to come from nowhere. In a matter of seconds the sea had turned from blue to purple, and billows of black cloud had blotted out the summer sky.

10 "Cut loose sheets, Dolores! We're carrying too much sail," Darcy shouted above the sound of creaking wood and snapping canvas. "Batten down the hatches! You and Dimanche man the lifeboat."

Dimanche's mother was nothing if not thorough, and it was her thoroughness, even in the face of mortal danger, that saved her baby daughter's life. She bundled Dimanche into her tiny

15 lifejacket, wrapped her in a blanket and tied her securely to the thwart. She kissed her, and turned towards her husband.

"Don't wait for me," he shouted. "I must belay the mizzen! You get in with Dimanche."

At that very moment, a monster of a wave, as strong as steel, rose high above the little boat, hung for a moment like a cliff of glass, and crashed on to the deck. It cracked the boat from stem to stern, splintered the mast, ripped through the sails, and tore baby Dimanche from her mother's arms, casting the lifeboat and its precious cargo adrift upon the sea.

Dimanche cried and struggled as the storm drove her fragile boat far to the south and west. All night the great waves surged, tossing the lifeboat like a cork. Salt sea spray soaked Dimanche's blanket, and an east wind turned her tiny face and hands to ice.

At dawn the next day, a fisherman from Kithira saw what he thought must be an empty lifeboat, rising and falling on the steady swell. He pulled in his net, and rowed across to take a look, hauling the battered lifeboat alongside with a boathook. Imagine his surprise when, looking in, he saw Dimanche, lying in a tangle of blanket in the bottom!

"Aphrodite, Goddess of Love and Beauty," he whispered, "who floated in her scallop shell past this very island, was not more beautiful than this child." Tearing off his jumper, he wrapped the baby in it and rowed for home, marvelling as he did so at the birthmark on the baby's wrist: it was just the shape of his own island of Kithira.

He and his wife were sorely tempted to keep the child, and how different this story would have been if they had done so. But they were parents themselves, and they could imagine all too well the frightful misery of this child's mother and father, if they were still alive. Sadly they gave her to the village priest, whose job it was to care for foundlings.

The priest took Dimanche by plane to Athens, on the mainland, and handed her over to the police. By this time the wreckage of the *Hippolytus* had been discovered, washed up on the coast of Milos. Helicopters were searching every square mile of sea from Samos down to Crete and northwards to the Sporades but neither Darcy nor Dolores was ever found.

The Greek police handed Dimanche over to someone from the Red Cross, who flew her back to London and placed her in the loving care of the Sisters of Small Mercies. In due course the following advertisement appeared in the personal column of *The Times*:

FOUND DRIFTING IN THE MEDITERRANEAN SEA, it said, DIMANCHE DILLER, BABY DAUGHTER OF DARCY AND DOLORES DILLER, BOTH BELIEVED LOST AT SEA.

[...]

If you are wondering how the nuns knew Dimanche's name, it was because her mother Dolores was so very thorough. She had sewn tiny embroidered name tapes into every one of Dimanche's clothes: her babygrow, her vest, her nappy, even her plastic pants, all bore her name in letters of pink silk.

1. What was the biggest 'cruel blow' that fate dealt Dimanche?

   A   The massive storm

   B   Being given to the village priest

   C   The shipwreck of their boat

   D   The loss of her parents

   E   The battering of the lifeboat

2. What saved Dimanche's life?

   A   Her mother's attention to detail

   B   The kindness of the village priest

   C   Her father's good sense

   D   Aphrodite, Goddess of Love and Beauty

   E   The actions of the Greek police

3. Which simile shows how high the 'monster of a wave' was that wrecked the *Hippolytus*?

   A   cracked the boat

   B   like a cliff of glass

   C   as strong as steel

   D   crashed on to the deck

   E   rose high above the little boat

4. Why didn't the fisherman and his wife keep Dimanche?

   A   The baby's birthmark was a sign of bad luck.

   B   They thought she should be returned to her parents.

   C   They already had enough children of their own.

   D   They knew the Greek police would arrest them.

   E   It was the village priest's job to care for foundlings.

5. Where were the remains of the Diller's boat found?

   A   Samos

   B   Crete

   C   Athens

   D   Milos

   E   The Sporades

(6) '...a wave, as strong as steel...' (line 18)

Which **two** literary techniques are used here?

A   Simile and onomatopoeia

B   Metaphor and simile

C   Alliteration and simile

D   Metaphor and personification

E   Personification and simile

(7) Which pronoun is used in the extract to address the reader?

A   They

B   Her

C   Me

D   Them

E   You

(8) What did the fisherman wrap Dimanche in?

A   A scallop shell

B   His jumper

C   A blanket

D   His arms

E   A life jacket

(9) 'casting the lifeboat and its precious cargo adrift upon the sea.' (line 21)

Which word is closest in meaning to 'cargo'?

A   Luggage

B   Lifeline

C   Goods

D   First-aid kit

E   Jewel

(10) The wave 'tore baby Dimanche from her mother's arms...' (lines 20–21)

Which literary technique is used here?

A   Personification

B   Alliteration

C   Simile

D   Metaphor

E   Hyperbole

Score: .... / 10

Spelling

In each question, circle the letter below the group of words containing a spelling mistake.

If there is no mistake, circle the letter N.

EXAMPLE

Jack used a cleer varnish to protect and strengthen the boat's teak deck.

(A)   B   C   D | N |

---

(1) My neighbour, whose name I can never remember, is always critisising me for being forgetful.

A   B   C   D | N |

(2) Xavier acheived world renown for his theatrical performances and musical compositions.

A   B   C   D | N |

(3) Although Beth meant well, she ended up being more of a hindrence to us than a help.

A   B   C   D | N |

(4) Anceint runes are characters scratched onto hard surfaces and consist

A   B   C

mostly of straight lines.

D | N |

(5) Our school secretery has scheduled an appointment for my parents to

A   B   C

meet with the governors.

D | N |

(6) The bargain hunters were determined to purchase flat-screen TVs in the 'sale of the centary'.

    A   B   C   D   **N**

(7) After a long bout of the flu, Nina did not feel equiped to compete against

    A   B   C

her rival in the contest.

    D   **N**

(8) Perry uses a physical assessment app to work out how many steps

    A   B   C

he covers on an avarage day.

    D   **N**

(9) The arrival of unexspected guests just as we were about to eat was quite inconvenient.

    A   B   C   D   **N**

(10) It has literally never ocurred to me to take the short cut through

    A   B   C

the fields to the leisure centre.

    D   **N**

(11) According to the media, the goverment's human rights policy is very controversial.

    A   B   C   D   **N**

(12) Although the weather was set to be changeable, Abi was determined they

    A   B   C

would eat on the terrace.

    D   **N**

Score: .... / 12

Punctuation

In each question, circle the letter below the group of words containing a punctuation mistake.

If there is no mistake, circle the letter **N**.

EXAMPLE

Brogan's little brother, who's called Joe scratched his best friend's new bike in the park today.

    A   **B**   **C**   **D**   **N**

---

① "Jade has eaten Granny," exclaimed Sadiq when Gran asked Jade if she'd like pizza.

    A   **B**   **C**   **D**   **N**

② The gingerbread cake recipe requires the following flour, eggs, butter, sugar and ginger.

    A   **B**   **C**   **D**   **N**

③ We like to go camping most weekends – even if it's raining but at the moment it's too cold.

    A   **B**   **C**   **D**   **N**

④ My thoughtful friend, whos coming round later, has always looked out for me in bad times.

    A   **B**   **C**   **D**   **N**

⑤ The gardeners keep their equipment in the sheds, which are always kept locked and alarmed.

    A   **B**   **C**   **D**   **N**

6 Maya couldn't've asked for a better brother (however, he does occasionally annoy her.

      A   B   C   D   **N**

7 We've been to Ireland, Wales, and Scotland but so far, we've never been to Spain.

      A   B   C   D   **N**

8 After a disappointing meal, we checked the bill only to find there was a big

      A   B   C

mistake what a surprise!

      D   **N**

9 As the wind increased the boat listed further over to port, resulting in the

      A   B   C

captain radioing for help.

      D   **N**

10 The children put on their hats coats and boots before going into

      A   B   C

the garden to build a snowman.

      D   **N**

11 My dad's window cleaning business has gone from strength to strength in the last, few weeks.

      A   B   C   D   **N**

12 There's been a further development in the case against well-known

      A   B   C

gang boss, Jim The King' Flynn.

      D   **N**

Score: .... / 12

In each question, circle the letter below the word or group of words that most accurately completes each sentence.

EXAMPLE

We decided to | parting | taken | participation | participate | part take | in the Spelling Bee.
            A   **B**   **C**   Ⓓ   **E**

① Dad's new spaghetti dish is better | as | for | than | of | then | any I've had before.
                    A **B**   **C**   **D**   **E**

② Bella | has ran | had ran | had run | run | has run | from school to the bus stop so she
        A   **B**   **C**   **D**   **E**

was exhausted.

③ It | was | is | can | ought | would | soon be time to pack up our tents and head home.
  A **B** **C** **D**   **E**

④ Abi approached the diving board but at the last minute, she got cold | hands | feet |
                                                     A   **B**

| fingers | toes | legs | .
  C   **D**   **E**

⑤ There are two new sections in the | childrens' | children | childs | childs' | children's |
                              A   **B**   **C**   **D**   **E**

library: comics and graphic novels.

⑥ Clare's mother, | that's | who's | what is | whose | which is | from Ireland, likes to
                A   **B**   **C**   **D**   **E**

read traditional tales.

(7) It was raining so we [bought] [brung] [brang] [brought] [bringed] the washing in.
                               A   B   C   D   E

(8) [Against] [Before] [Through] [With] [After] all the odds, Victor won the
     A   B   C   D   E

skiing competition.

(9) Relaxing in the garden on a summer's day is very [satisfy] [satisfying] [satisfied]
                                            A   B   C

[satisfaction] [dissatisfied] .
     D   E

(10) [At] [With] [Under] [In] [For] no time at all, the firefighters had extinguished the
   A   B   C   D   E

flames and made the area safe.

(11) Myla [litt] [lightened] [lit] [light] [lighten] the candles then brought the cake in to
         A   B   C   D   E

her little brother.

(12) After [having ate] [have eaten] [have ate] [have been eaten] [having eaten] ,
        A   B   C   D   E

Bethany watched TV.

Score: .... / 12

Comprehension

Read the text below and answer the questions that follow. In each question, circle the letter next to the correct answer.

EXAMPLE

Nicolas's eyes were the size of dinner plates when he saw the number of presents under the Christmas tree.

Which adjective best describes how Nicolas was feeling?

A   Furious

(B)   Excited

C   Afraid

D   Jealous

E   Frightened

The following is an extract from the poem 'The Highwayman' by Alfred Noyes

PART ONE

The wind was a torrent of darkness among the gusty trees.
The moon was a ghostly galleon tossed upon cloudy seas.
The road was a ribbon of moonlight over the purple moor,
And the highwayman came riding—
5   Riding—riding—
The highwayman came riding, up to the old inn-door.

He'd a French cocked-hat on his forehead, a bunch of lace at his chin,
A coat of the claret velvet, and breeches of brown doe-skin.
They fitted with never a wrinkle. His boots were up to the thigh.
10 And he rode with a jewelled twinkle,
                His pistol butts a-twinkle,
His rapier hilt a-twinkle, under the jewelled sky.

Over the cobbles he clattered and clashed in the dark inn-yard.
He tapped with his whip on the shutters, but all was locked and barred.
15 He whistled a tune to the window, and who should be waiting there
But the landlord's black-eyed daughter,
              Bess, the landlord's daughter,
Plaiting a dark red love-knot into her long black hair.

"One kiss, my bonny sweetheart, I'm after a prize to-night,

20 But I shall be back with the yellow gold before the morning light;

Yet, if they press me sharply, and harry me through the day,

Then look for me by moonlight,

Watch for me by moonlight,

I'll come to thee by moonlight, though hell should bar the way."

PART TWO

25 He did not come in the dawning. He did not come at noon;

And out of the tawny sunset, before the rise of the moon,

When the road was a gypsy's ribbon, looping the purple moor,

A red-coat troop came marching—

Marching—marching—

30 King George's men came marching, up to the old inn-door.

They said no word to the landlord. They drank his ale instead.

But they gagged his daughter, and bound her, to the foot of her narrow bed.

Two of them knelt at her casement, with muskets at their side!

There was death at every window;

35 And hell at one dark window;

For Bess could see, through her casement, the road that *he* would ride.

They had tied her up to attention, with many a sniggering jest.

She twisted her hands behind her; but all the knots held good!

She writhed her hands till her fingers were wet with sweat or blood!

40 They stretched and strained in the darkness, and the hours crawled by like years

Till, now, on the stroke of midnight,

Cold, on the stroke of midnight,

The tip of one finger touched it! The trigger at least was hers!

The tip of one finger touched it. She strove no more for the rest.

45 Up, she stood up to attention, with the muzzle beneath her breast.

She would not risk their hearing; she would not strive again;

For the road lay bare in the moonlight;

Blank and bare in the moonlight;

And the blood of her veins, in the moonlight, throbbed to her love's refrain.

50 *Tlot-tlot*, in the frosty silence! *Tlot-tlot*, in the echoing night!

Nearer he came and nearer. Her face was like a light.

Her eyes grew wide for a moment; she drew one last deep breath,

Then her finger moved in the moonlight,

Her musket shattered the moonlight,

55 Shattered her breast in the moonlight and warned him—with her death.

He turned. He spurred to the west; he did not know who stood

Bowed, with her head o'er the musket, drenched with her own blood!

Not till the dawn he heard it, and his face grew grey to hear

How Bess, the landlord's daughter,

60 The landlord's black-eyed daughter,

Had watched for her love in the moonlight, and died in the darkness there.

1. What does the second verse tell you about the highwayman?

    A   He is dressed like a soldier.

    B   He has good fashion sense and is well-to-do.

    C   He is poor and scruffy.

    D   He is an arrogant show-off.

    E   He is good-looking and kind.

2. Why does the highwayman whistle when he gets into the inn-yard?

    A   To get the landlord's attention

    B   To get the horse's attention

    C   To get Bess's attention

    D   To show how tuneful he is

    E   To alert the soldiers

3. 'I'm after a prize to-night,' (line 19)

    What do you think his 'prize' is?

    A   The gold he is planning to steal

    B   King George's men

    C   The landlord's ale

    D   Bess's long black hair

    E   A dark red love-knot

4. 'They had tied her up to attention, ...' (line 37)

    What is meant by tying Bess 'up to attention'?

    A   She was tied bolt upright so she could see through the window.

    B   They made sure she paid attention to what they were doing.

    C   They paid a lot of attention to how they tied her up.

    D   They made sure the other soldiers were paying attention.

    E   She was tied to the chair so she didn't slide off.

5. When did the highwayman learn of Bess's death?

    A   The following week

    B   In the early morning

    C   That evening

    D   In the middle of the night

    E   He never heard about it.

(6) '*Tlot-tlot*, in the frosty silence! *Tlot-tlot*, in the echoing night!' (line 50)

Which literary technique is used in this line?

A   Sarcasm

B   Simile

C   Idiom

D   Hyperbole

E   Onomatopoeia

(7) 'Then her finger moved in the moonlight,' (line 53)

What was the result of Bess moving her finger?

A   She waved at the highwayman.

B   She shot the soldiers.

C   She could wipe away her blood.

D   She was able to pull the trigger.

E   She cut free of her ties.

(8) 'she would not strive again;' (line 46)

Which word below is closest in meaning to 'strive'?

A   Love

B   Struggle

C   Stand

D   Care

E   Speak

(9) What type of poem is 'The Highwayman'?

A   Sonnet

B   Haiku

C   Limerick

D   Ode

E   Ballad

(10) Which literary device is used in each of the first three lines of the first verse?

A   Simile

B   Personification

C   Alliteration

D   Metaphor

E   Onomatopoeia

Score: .... / 10

Spelling

In each question, circle the letter below the group of words containing a spelling mistake.

If there is no mistake, circle the letter **N**.

EXAMPLE

Jack used a cleer varnish to protect and strengthen the boat's teak deck.

   (A)   B   C   D   **N**

---

(1) The construction work in our town is causing major traffic disruption,

       A   **B**   **C**

which is very inconvienient.

       D   **N**

(2) Gregor felt harrassed when the person behind him in the queue

       A   **B**   **C**

repeatedly told him to move on.

       D   **N**

(3) The winning team were consious that they had yet to show their appreciation to their coach.

       A   **B**   **C**   **D** **N**

(4) Battered and briused from the karate competition, Ben especially looked

       A   **B**   **C**

forward to a soak in the bath.

       D   **N**

5. May had expected the debate to be controversial but she hadn't barganed

   A   B   C

   on aggressive behaviour.

   D   N

6. I find that keeping a dictionery close to hand is very beneficial when I'm reading and writing.

   A   B   C   D   N

7. "Curiosity killed the cat," said Mum when she caught me reading my sister's correspondence.

   A   B   C   D   N

8. In science, we had to identify liquids, solids and gases, and place

   A   B   C

   them into relevant catagories.

   D   N

9. There was an akward silence as Ginny revealed she had spilt nail varnish

   A   B   C

   over Mum's new blouse.

   D   N

10. Yen, who is eight, was a nusance when he accompanied me and my friends to the museum.

    A   B   C   D   N

11. According to my dad, if we plan a camping trip, the weather is garanteed to be disastrous.

    A   B   C   D   N

12. "Three twelths is the same as one quarter," said Jamail, interrupting the teacher in our lesson.

    A   B   C   D   N

Score: .... / 12

Test	# Punctuation
15	You have 6 minutes to complete this test.
	You have 12 questions to complete within the time given.

In each question, circle the letter below the group of words containing a punctuation mistake.

If there is no mistake, circle the letter N.

EXAMPLE

Brogan's little brother, who's called Joe scratched his best friend's new bike in the park today.

  A   **(B)**   **C**   **D**   **N**

---

① With no time to lose, Cal released the handbrake, put his foot down and

  A   **B**   **C**

sped, off into the distance.

  D   **N**

② At first we thought Flo was rather rude but after a few weeks, she revealed her nicer side.

  A   **B**   **C**   **D**   **N**

③ "It's time we replaced the toaster," said Dad, "That's the third time

  A   **B**   **C**

this week I've had burnt toast!"

  D   **N**

④ "What a surprise?" exclaimed Josh. "I really didn't expect a brand-new bike for my birthday."

  A   **B**   **C**   **D**   **N**

⑤ The problem with Jake is undoubtedly this he doesn't know when

  A   **B**   **C**

to stop teasing his brother.

  D   **N**

6. My mother, who qualified as a teacher only last year, now has

     A   B   C

a job at Hillgate Primary school.

     D   **N**

7. There are many reasons why I don't know my times tables but no one will listen to me

     A   B   C   D   **N**

8. I'd been looking for new skis for ages so I was delighted, when a pair

     A   B   C

popped up on the internet.

     D   **N**

9. Rajiv and Paul have said they'd like to go go-kart racing next week

     A   B   C

but I'm unable to join them.

     D   **N**

10. I expect we'll see Gena and Thea later so I'll tell them then that I shant be

     A   B   C

able to go to their show.

     D   **N**

11. "You don't understand how serious the situation is, do you." said the

     A   B   C

police officer to the thief.

     D   **N**

12. Three times I've asked Ralf to help me three times he's refused. What

     A   B   C

am I going to do with him?

     D   **N**

Score: .... / 12

Sentence Completion

You have 6 minutes to complete this test.

You have 12 questions to complete within the time given.

In each question, circle the letter below the word or group of words that most accurately completes each sentence.

EXAMPLE

We decided to | **parting** | **taken** | **participation** | **participate** | **part take** | in the Spelling Bee.
               A   B   C   Ⓓ   E

---

① The bells | **were rung** | **were rang** | **had been rang** | **was rung** | **have rang**
             A   B   C   D   E

to celebrate the new year.

② No one had expected thunder and | **lightening** | **lightnen** | **lighten** | **lighting** | **lightning**
                        A   B   C   D   E

at the music festival.

③ The book, | **what** | **which** | **whom** | **where** | **when** | won the Booker Prize, is about a
            A   B   C   D   E

family on a desert island.

④ Jude found it hard not to | **medal** | **meddel** | **meddle** | **metal** | **mettle** | in other
                   A   B   C   D   E

people's business.

⑤ Monty, my Labrador, | **was laying** | **has laid** | **did lay** | **was lying** | **was lied** | on his
               A   B   C   D   E

bed, breathing heavily after his walk.

6 Chang was no angel but better the devil [you know] [you don't know] [you didn't know]

　　　　　　　　　　　　　　　　　　　　　A　　　　　**B**　　　　　　　**C**

[who knows] [whose nose] .

　　D　　　　　**E**

7 Gretchen got her spellings [alright] [allright] [altogether] [all right] [all write] .

　　　　　　　　　　　　　　　A　　　**B**　　　　**C**　　　　　**D**　　　　**E**

8 Margie found it hard to [effect] [accept] [precept] [except] [affect] that she would

　　　　　　　　　　　　　　A　　　　**B**　　　　**C**　　　**D**　　　**E**

soon be moving to America.

9 Ciaran is [immigrating] [emanating] [migrating] [emerging] [emigrating]

　　　　　　　　　A　　　　　　**B**　　　　　　**C**　　　　　**D**　　　　　**E**

from England to America next year.

10 The carnival [preceded] [processed] [proceeded] [probated] [proacted]

　　　　　　　　　A　　　　　　**B**　　　　　**C**　　　　　**D**　　　　**E**

down the main road, much to the delight of the crowds.

11 Pia's [reference] [preference] [preferral] [referal] [conference] to the school

　　　　　A　　　　　　**B**　　　　　**C**　　　　**D**　　　　**E**

fair sparked an immediate flurry of excitement.

12 The climbers decided to make the [decent] [ascent] [descent] [assent] [accent]

　　　　　　　　　　　　　　　　　　　A　　　**B**　　　　**C**　　　　**D**　　　**E**

to the top of the summit at first light.

Read the text below and answer the questions that follow. In each question, circle the letter next to the correct answer.

EXAMPLE

Nicolas's eyes were the size of dinner plates when he saw the number of presents under the Christmas tree.

Which adjective best describes how Nicolas was feeling?

A   Furious

(B)   Excited

C   Afraid

D   Jealous

E   Frightened

The following is an extract from *Last Hours on Everest* by Graham Hoyland

George Mallory was an English mountaineer who participated in the first three British Mount Everest expeditions. During an expedition in 1924, Mallory and his Everest climbing partner disappeared. Graham Hoyland, who in 1993 became the fifteenth Englishman to climb Everest, was obsessed with finding their bodies.

Chapter 1
Start of an Obsession

Mountaineering is in my blood. My father started taking me out into the hills of Arran when I was five, and I can still remember the moment when we scrambled to the top of the island's highest mountain. I saw the sea laid out almost three thousand feet beneath us like a polished steel floor. Down there was Brodick Bay, with the ferry steaming in from the mainland like a
5   toy boat.

Climbing was filled with sensation: the sheer agony of panting up steep slopes in the summer sun, the sharp smell of my father's sweat as we lay resting in the heather, the hard coldness of a swim in the burn. Then the gritty feel of the granite under your fingers, and the blast of wind in your face as you breasted the summit.

10   It must have been a double-edged pleasure for my father, though. His brother, John Hoyland had been killed on Mont Blanc in 1934. Jack Longland, a famous climber of the day who was on the 1933 Everest expedition, described John as 'potentially the best mountaineer of his

generation … there was no young English climber since George Mallory of whom it seemed safe to expect so much'.

15 John had hoped to go on the next expedition to Everest, but his death at the age of nineteen had put paid to those hopes. Even I could feel the loss at thirty years' distance.

My father told me about another climbing hero in our family, a man who had been close to the summit of Mount Everest in 1924. He called him 'Uncle Hunch', and Dad said that one day I would meet him. He said he'd been a close friend of George Mallory, and again that name
20 was mentioned. Mallory, the paragon of climbers. My young mind took it all in.

[…]

Eventually, when I was 13 and he was 81, I met Uncle Hunch.

[…]

He really was an extraordinarily gifted man: a double first at Cambridge, a talented artist (his pictures of Everest are still on the walls of the Alpine Club) and an accomplished musician (he transcribed the music he heard in Tibet into Western notation). He served as an army
25 surgeon during the First World War and was one of the foremost alpinists of the day when he was invited to join the 1922 Mount Everest expedition. He took part in the first serious attempt to climb the mountain, and his oxygen-free height record stood for over 50 years. General C. G. Bruce, the expedition leader, described his strength on the mountain: 'Stands by himself … an extraordinary capacity for going day after day.'

[…]

30 At that stage in my life I knew nothing about this, I was only interested in the incredible story he was telling me. He was a stout old man by then, with the slight stoop that gave him his family name, but his voice still contained the excitement of his twenties youth.

'Norton and I had a last-ditch attempt to climb Mount Everest, and we got higher than any man had ever been before. I really couldn't breathe properly and on the way down my throat
35 blocked up completely. I sat down to die, but as one last try I pressed my chest hard' – and here the old man pushed his chest to demonstrate to his fascinated audience – 'and up came the blockage. We got down safely. We met Mallory at the North Col on his way up. He said to me that he had forgotten his camera, and I lent him mine. So, if my camera was ever found,' said Uncle Hunch to me, 'you could prove that Mallory got to the top.' It was a throw-away
40 comment that he probably had made a hundred times in the course of telling this story, but this time it found its mark.

---

(1) 'Climbing was filled with sensation' (line 6)
Which three noun phrases below does Graham use to describe the sensations he experienced when climbing with his father?

A   steep slopes, the heather, swim in the burn

B   sheer agony, sharp smell, gritty feel

C   blast of wind, under your fingers, father's sweat

D   swim in the burn, in your face, steep slopes

E   double-edged pleasure, summer sun, resting in the heather

(2) What does Graham mean by, 'It must have been a double-edged pleasure for my father...'? (line 10)

A   His father lost his love of climbing after his brother's death.

B   There were two different kinds of pleasure to climbing for his dad.

C   His father loved climbing but it was a sad reminder of his brother's death.

D   The 'double-edged' pleasure refers to John Hoyland and Jack Longland.

E   His father enjoyed climbing twice as much after his brother's death.

(3) Which statement about Uncle Hunch below is **not** true?

A   He was an accomplished musician.

B   He joined the 1922 Everest expedition.

C   He was the paragon of climbers.

D   He had been a close friend of George Mallory.

E   Along with John, he was a family climbing hero.

(4) What saved Uncle Hunch from certain death?

A   He got help from George Mallory.

B   He took some medicine to clear his throat.

C   He descended the summit when it got too dangerous.

D   He cleared the blockage in his throat.

E   He ditched his attempt to climb Everest.

(5) Who led the expedition in 1922?

A   Norton

B   Jack Longland

C   Uncle Hunch

D   George Mallory

E   General Bruce

(6) '...the sheer agony of panting up steep slopes in the summer sun, the sharp smell of my father's sweat ...' (lines 6–7)

Which literary technique is used here?

A   Alliteration

B   Metaphor

C   Simile

D   Personification

E   Onomatopoeia

7 Read the paragraph starting, 'He really was an extraordinarily gifted man...'.

Which **three adjectives** best describe Uncle Hunch?

Option 1: talented

Option 2: determined

Option 3: serious

Option 4: strong

    A   Options 1 and 3 only

    B   Options 2 and 4 only

    C   Options 1 and 4 only

    D   Options 1, 2 and 4 only

    E   Options 1, 2 and 3 only

8 What would be the significance if Uncle Hunch's camera were found?

    A   It might prove that Mallory had got to the top.

    B   It would prove Mallory had met Uncle Hunch.

    C   It would show that Mallory hadn't returned the camera.

    D   It would prove that Mallory had forgotten his camera.

    E   It might show that Mallory was still alive.

9 'I saw the sea laid out almost three thousand feet beneath us like a polished steel floor.' (lines 3–4)

Which literary technique is used here?

    A   Metaphor

    B   Simile

    C   Rhetoric

    D   Personification

    E   Alliteration

10 Which of the following is a synonym of 'foremost'? (line 25)

    A   Leading

    B   Interesting

    C   Competitive

    D   Alternative

    E   Successful

Score: .... / 10

Test	Spelling
18	You have 6 minutes to complete this test. You have 12 questions to complete within the time given.

In each question, circle the letter below the group of words containing a spelling mistake.

If there is no mistake, circle the letter N.

EXAMPLE

Jack used a cleer varnish to protect and strengthen the boat's teak deck.

Ⓐ   B   C   D   N

---

1 Gerry is an excellent amature boxer who is determined to turn professional in due course.

A   B   C   D   N

2 Each individual in my class is privileged to have warm clothing and sufficient nutritious food.

A   B   C   D   N

3 My teacher frequently sacrifises her break to give me the opportunity

A   B   C

to practise my spelling.

D   N

4 When you get anxious, it is recommended to breathe in and out in a steady ryhthm.

A   B   C   D   N

5 The poppy, though not compulsory, is worn as a symble of remembrance

A   B   C

of those who died in war.

D   N

6 Florence is renowned for her competetive nature, especially when it
      A   **B**   **C**

comes to physical activities.
     D   **N**

7 Orla, who has emigrated to Italy, struggles with the pronounciation of
      A   **B**   **C**

certain tricky Italian words.
     D   **N**

8 In a desperate attempt to get the celebrity's autograph, the fans joined the lengthy cue.
      A   **B**   **C**   **D**   **N**

9 Parlament has today approved the new policy but it will be several
      A   **B**   **C**

months before it becomes law.
     D   **N**

10 The technical department explained to the committee that there had been
      A   **B**   **C**

numerous systym failures.
     D   **N**

11 Tee was embarassed when he was singled out as the highest achieving
      A   **B**   **C**

mathematician in his class.
     D   **N**

12 The inmates have apparently alleged that they were repeatedly subjected
      A   **B**   **C**

to prejidice in prison.
     D   **N**

Score: .... / 12

Punctuation

In each question, circle the letter below the group of words containing a punctuation mistake.

If there is no mistake, circle the letter N.

EXAMPLE

Brogan's little brother, who's called Joe scratched his best friend's new bike in the park today.

| | A | | B | | C | | D | | N |

---

1 The mens' changing rooms have been demolished and the new ones will be

    A   B   C

finished in the spring.

    D   **N**

2 Sadie says that it won't be long until all our homework is online

    A   B   C

and our pens' become redundant!

    D   **N**

3 It was a pleasure to meet Val from Chester; Roy from Poole; Lee

    A   B   C

from Hull; and Sally from Sale.

    D   **N**

4 Clara and Fred said theyre going to meet us at the park at eleven o'clock

    A   B   C

so don't be late, please.

    D   **N**

(5) Frantically looking for the missing key Chai resolved he'd never get into

      A   **B**   **C**

such a predicament again.

      D   **N**

(6) The main attraction at the School fair was throwing balloons filled with water at Mr Toms.

      A   **B**   **C**   **D**   **N**

(7) Mum reads my brother a nursery rhyme at bedtime his favourite is Humpty Dumpty.

      A   **B**   **C**   **D**   **N**

(8) We shouldn't laugh at Aunty Jess new hat although I know it's rather

      A   **B**   **C**

comical with the feather.

      D   **N**

(9) Winnie is really looking forward to the new performing arts theatre,

      A   **B**   **C**

which opens in the Summer.

      D   **N**

(10) "Have you seen Monty? Jon asked, a concerned expression on his face.

      A   **B**   **C**

"He's been gone for ages."

      D   **N**

(11) If you'd like to apply for the position of school councillor then please

      A   **B**   **C**

contact the head teacher.

      D   **N**

(12) "Why on earth you think I have your book, I really don't know?"

      A   **B**   **C**

said Frank, shrugging dramatically.

      D   **N**

Score: .... / 12

Sentence Completion

You have 6 minutes to complete this test.

You have 12 questions to complete within the time given.

In each question, circle the letter below the word or group of words that most accurately completes each sentence.

EXAMPLE

We decided to | **parting** | **taken** | **participation** | **participate** | **part take** | in the Spelling Bee.
A   B   C   Ⓓ   E

① The place | **were** | **we're** | **where** | **wear** | **weir** | we had arranged to meet was halfway
A   B   C   D   E

between the town centre and school.

② Marcus | **answered** | **said** | **required** | **asked** | **exclaimed** | his mum if they could go
A   B   C   D   E

to the cinema at the weekend.

③ The scout captain | **lead** | **led** | **leads** | **laid** | **leaded** | us deep into the forest where we
A   B   C   D   E

pitched our tents.

④ Jaime was always very | **through** | **though** | **thought** | **trough** | **thorough** | when it
A   B   C   D   E

came to revising for his exams.

⑤ " | **Whom** | **Who** | **What** | **Which** | **Why** | did Mac choose as his partner for the
A   B   C   D   E

school trip?" asked Kim.

6. Yolande [past]_A [passed]_B [pass]_C [pasted]_D [passes]_E the book to Archie when the teacher

wasn't looking.

7. "It's late, so we really should head home; [beside the point]_A [bedside]_B [beset]_C

[besides]_D [beside]_E , it's raining," remarked Theo wisely.

8. "If we [take]_A [hadn't taken]_B [had took]_C [hadn't took]_D [took]_E the coastal route, we'd

be there by now," moaned Jo.

9. Those books aren't ours, they are [there's]_A [they'res]_B [theirs]_C [their's]_D [theres]_E ,"

said Ronan.

10. There was a meeting of the [council]_A [counsel]_B [cancel]_C [cancellation]_D [counselling]_E

to discuss the latest issues.

11. Philippa doesn't approve [on]_A [with]_B [of]_C [for]_D [at]_E eating animals or hunting them

for their fur.

12. Next year, [we'd been]_A [we've been]_B [we went]_C [we have gone]_D [we're going]_E

to go camping in the Scottish Highlands.

Score: .... / 12

53

Read the text below and answer the questions that follow. In each question, circle the letter next to the correct answer.

EXAMPLE

Nicolas's eyes were the size of dinner plates when he saw the number of presents under the Christmas tree.

Which adjective best describes how Nicolas was feeling?

A   Furious

(B)   Excited

C   Afraid

D   Jealous

E   Frightened

The following is an extract from 'St John: Turtle Soup' by travel writer James Draven

"Who wants to bet on how long it will take us to see turtles?" asks Paul Askew, our kayaking guide, smirking through his heavy beard. His eyes are twinkling with mischievousness in the sunlight, as we pull our vessels up onto the retina-scorching white sands of Scott Beach on the island of St John. I can tell from his wry wagering that we're going to be in for a treat.
5   Eventually, he lets his us in on the joke: "It's never taken me more than five minutes to find turtles when I take groups snorkelling here!"

Two thirds of St John, a US territory in the Caribbean, is designated as the Virgin Islands National Park, which protects over a hundred archaeological sites dating from as early as 840 BC to the arrival of Columbus in 1493. It's also a haven for wildlife and, since arriving in the national park by
10   rigid inflatable boat from Cruz Bay, I've been kayaking around with Paul, visiting the stunning swathes at Honeymoon Beach, and the six-foot-long tarpon fish that ply Henley Cay. I've been awaiting the main event: snorkelling in Scott Beach Bay, an area that reputedly teems with sea turtles.

20 minutes later, Paul is looking a little red-faced, and not just because of the blazing sunshine: we've been snorkelling around – arching out into the deep and back, from one end of the beach
15   to the other – and seen nothing. The water is as warm as the toddlers' pool at your local swimming baths, and almost certainly cleaner, but despite the crystalline visibility, nobody has seen anything but delicately rippled white sand on the seabed.

We turn to take a second lap of the waters and, as we cut through the middle of the circle we've just swum, we finally spot two hawksbill turtles on the bottom, munching on a few
20   scant clumps of seagrass.

"We must have snorkelled right around them," laughs Paul, realising our quarry has been at the centre of our orbit, forming the hub of the wheel we've just spent nearly half an hour plotting.

Within a few minutes, the rest of my group heads for shore, satisfied with their turtle sighting, but just as I'm hanging back to get a final look at the turtles, another drifts by, being tailed
25 by a large remora fish. The remora has an in-built sucker which enables it to ride along atop the turtle's shell, removing ectoparasites, getting a free ride, and feeding on its host's scraps and faeces. When I dive down to take a closer look at their mutual relationship, the fish darts underneath the turtle's body, sharing its protective shell.

Spellbound, I follow the turtle's tranquil trajectory through the water, and then suddenly I'm
30 surrounded. The water is thick with turtles of all sizes. They flap past me, languid and hypnotic, as I bob around in this bewitching broth, limp-limbed in the calm, cradling currents of these serene seas.

The turtle tracked by the remora takes a course directly beneath me for a while, swimming along in my shadow before she starts to rise up towards me until she's just a foot from my
35 face, her shell gliding by my snorkel mask glass. Amid the patterns and patina of her shell, the mottled hues of greens and browns, there's a faint design visible through the clear water, like a tribal tattoo, Maori markings inked almost imperceptibly on her back.

Then she pops up out of the water in front of me as I stop to give her space. She considers me for a second, takes a gulp of air then dives back down, swimming beside me and seemingly
40 scrutinising my very being with eyes that disappear into eternity. I stare back in awe, mesmerised, fully comprehending the minds of the ancient Hindu storytellers who wrote myths of the Cosmic Turtle that carried the world on its back.

In this trance, I follow as she dives down towards the seabed, leaving the throng of her tribe behind, with the remora at her belly and me directly behind: a zen procession into the deep,
45 following my sub-mariner soul mate.

Just then, she releases an enormous stream of her own soup, stewing me in a miasma of abhorrent bouillabaisse. Obviously, she thinks I'm just another sucker.

---

(1) Why does the kayaking guide smirk when he asks: "Who wants to bet on how long it will take us to see turtles?" (line 1)

   A   Because he likes making bets with the visitors

   B   Because it has never taken more than five minutes

   C   Because he knows that they won't see any turtles

   D   Because snorkelling groups tend to scare off turtles

   E   Because he always wins any wagers he makes

Questions continue on next page

(2) How many years old are the archaeological sites on St John?

A   Over two thousand

B   Eight hundred and forty

C   One thousand, four hundred and ninety-three

D   Over three thousand

E   Around one thousand

(3) What is it that James is particularly looking forward to on St John?

A   Visiting Honeymoon Beach

B   Kayaking with Paul, the guide

C   Seeing the six-foot-long tarpon fish

D   Taking the inflatable to Cruz Bay

E   Snorkelling in Scott Beach Bay

(4) Why is Paul 'looking a little red-faced'? (line 13)

Option 1: The heat from the sun

Option 2: He's over-exerted himself.

Option 3: He's embarrassed as they've not seen any turtles.

Option 4: He has a temperature.

A   Option 1 only

B   Options 2 and 4

C   Options 2 and 3

D   Options 1 and 3

E   Option 3 only

(5) How does the remora fish benefit from the turtle?

A   The remora removes ectoparasites.

B   The turtle shows the remora where to find food.

C   The remora gets a free ride, food and protection.

D   The turtle allows the remora to share its habitat.

E   The remora is camouflaged against the turtle's shell.

(6) Read the paragraph beginning 'Spellbound…' again.

Which adjective tells us that there are an exceptional number of turtles?

A   Tranquil

B   Cradling

C   Languid

D   Bewitching

E   Thick

(7) 'she releases an enormous stream of her own soup' (line 46)

What does James mean?

A   The turtle defecates.

B   The turtle is sick.

C   The turtle ejects a special ink.

D   The turtle creates a soupy current.

E   The turtle releases venom.

(8) 'I've been awaiting the main event: snorkelling in Scott Beach Bay, an area that reputedly teems with sea turtles.' (lines 11–12)

Which definition is closest in meaning to 'reputedly'?

A   Without doubt

B   Instantly

C   Allegedly

D   According to general belief

E   In past times

(9) What simile does James use to describe the water they are swimming in?

A   the crystalline visibility

B   the toddlers' pool at your local swimming baths

C   the calm, cradling currents

D   retina-scorching white sands

E   a zen procession into the deep

(10) 'I follow as she dives down towards the seabed, leaving the throng of her tribe behind, with the remora at her belly and me directly behind: a zen procession into the deep,' (lines 43–44)

Which literary technique is used here?

A   Personification

B   Simile

C   Rhetoric

D   Metaphor

E   Onomatopoeia

Score: .... / 10

Spelling

In each question, circle the letter below the group of words containing a spelling mistake.

If there is no mistake, circle the letter **N**.

EXAMPLE

Jack used a cleer varnish to protect and strengthen the boat's teak deck.

(A)   B   C   D | N |

---

1 Ellis is currently working as a foriegn correspondent for an international news agency.

A   B   C   D | N |

2 According to the media, the new legislation is likely to provoke intense

A   B   C

political controversy.

D | N |

3 Ronnie's apology was cincere – he truly hadn't intended to kick the

A   B   C

ball towards Fay's stomach.

D | N |

4 It wasn't exactly a life, Tom decided; it was merely an existense,

A   B   C

but how much could he endure?

D | N |

(5) A huge argument developped about the pollution emanating from the chemical plant.

      A   B   C   D   **N**

(6) My family and I are very familier with the array of characters in all the Harry Potter films.

      A   B   C   D   **N**

(7) The website indicated that the trousers were not availible in my preferred colour or my size.

      A   B   C   D   **N**

(8) Dr Well, a respected member of the medical profesion, is unperturbed

      A   B   C

by jokes about his name.

      D   **N**

(9) The principle of the college announced that he was retiring and intended to live abroad.

      A   B   C   D   **N**

(10) When Bea and Todd argue, it's best not to interfear as they

      A   B   C

usually resolve the situation themselves.

      D   **N**

(11) Fleur resides in a borogh of London, not far from a medieval castle and a huge fortress.

      A   B   C   D   **N**

(12) The head looked very solem as she announced that a thief had broken into school overnight.

      A   B   C   D   **N**

Score: .... / 12

Test	**Punctuation**
23	You have 6 minutes to complete this test. You have 12 questions to complete within the time given.

In each question, circle the letter below the group of words containing a punctuation mistake.

If there is no mistake, circle the letter **N**.

EXAMPLE

Brogan's little brother, who's called Joe scratched his best friend's new bike in the park today.

A   Ⓑ   C   D   N

---

1 Beth was excited about sharing her new dish with her friends; spaghetti

A   B   C

carbonara and garlic bread.

D   N

2 The trucks rear wheel hit a kerb and before we knew it, it had overturned in the road.

A   B   C   D   N

3 Shamelessly Robbie cheekily told the new teacher that her shoes looked

A   B   C

odd with her new dress.

D   N

4 We knew we'd won the tournament it was just a case of whether we'd won the league.

A   B   C   D   N

5 As we filed into assembly, it became apparent from the teachers faces

A   B   C

that something was amiss.

D   N

(6) Maria likes long walks in the countryside but her sister prefers the hustle

      A   B   C

and bustle of the city.

      D   [N]

(7) "Let's talk about Dad's surprise birthday party" said Leah excitedly.

      A   B   C

"We haven't got long to plan."

      D   [N]

(8) On Christmas day, we generally open our presents early in the morning

      A   B   C

then we have a big breakfast.

      D   [N]

(9) Carrots and parsnips are Jamals two favourite vegetables, though

      A   B   C

asparagus is a close runner-up.

      D   [N]

(10) Clara's hoping that shell be able to go travelling when she's finished her university course.

      A   B   C   D   [N]

(11) For the last two years Joe has been working as a geologist in the Australian uranium mines.

      A   B   C   D   [N]

(12) Ursula's just come back from the shop; she bought a box of Golden crunch for breakfast.

      A   B   C   D   [N]

Score: .... / 12

In each question, circle the letter below the word or group of words that most accurately completes each sentence.

EXAMPLE

We decided to | **parting** | **taken** | **participation** | **participate** | **part take** | in the Spelling Bee.

A B C (D) E

(1) Therese has always succeeded | **that** | **with** | **for** | **of** | **in** | everything she turns her hand to.

    A B C D E

(2) Gina had to stay after school | **although** | **before** | **even** | **because** | **why** | she

         A   B   C   D   E

had misbehaved.

(3) The job | **what** | **which** | **for** | **where** | **whichever** | Mum has applied for would mean

     A   B C   D   E

relocating to London.

(4) It's been raining cats and | **kittens** | **puppies** | **elephants** | **crocodiles** | **dogs** | all day.

        A   B   C   D   E

(5) The monarch's | **courtiers** | **curtains** | **croutons** | **courteous** | **cretins** | attend to his

       A   B   C   D   E

every need.

(6) Dario | **favoured** | **is favoured** | **favours** | **favourite** | **flavours** | holidays by the sea

    A   B   C   D   E

but his sister prefers the mountains.

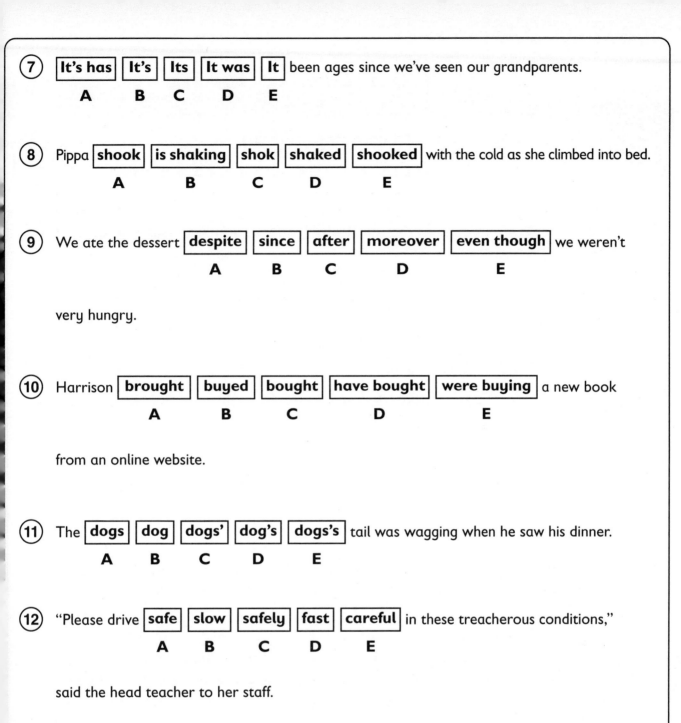

(7) | It's has | It's | Its | It was | It | been ages since we've seen our grandparents.

   A   B   C   D   E

(8) Pippa | shook | is shaking | shok | shaked | shooked | with the cold as she climbed into bed.

   A   B   C   D   E

(9) We ate the dessert | despite | since | after | moreover | even though | we weren't

   A   B   C   D   E

very hungry.

(10) Harrison | brought | buyed | bought | have bought | were buying | a new book

   A   B   C   D   E

from an online website.

(11) The | dogs | dog | dogs' | dog's | dogs's | tail was wagging when he saw his dinner.

   A   B   C   D   E

(12) "Please drive | safe | slow | safely | fast | careful | in these treacherous conditions,"

   A   B   C   D   E

said the head teacher to her staff.

Score: .... / 12

63

Comprehension

You have 10 minutes to complete this test.

You have 10 questions to complete within the time given.

Read the text below and answer the questions that follow. In each question, circle the letter next to the correct answer.

EXAMPLE

Nicolas's eyes were the size of dinner plates when he saw the number of presents under the Christmas tree.

Which adjective best describes how Nicolas was feeling?

A   Furious   **B**   Excited   C   Afraid

D   Jealous   E   Frightened

The following is an extract from *Finding Bear* by Hannah Gold

When April and her father had first arrived back from the Arctic, it had been like diving into the deep end of a very cold swimming pool. The constant noise and smog of cars and motorbikes, with their never-ending stench of exhaust, had been the most horrible shock. And *people*. So many people everywhere. Hustling, bustling and jostling every crowded minute of the day.

5   It had been Dad's decision to hasten the move to the seaside and within a month, they had sold their tall and gloomy city house and found somewhere new near Granny Apples. It wasn't necessarily the kind of house April would have chosen herself. Number Thirty-Four, Stirling Road sat in a row of identical modern red-brick houses, each with its own neatly lawned back garden and freshly painted fence. Unlike their old home, or even the wooden cabin on Bear

10   Island, this house was filled with hard, square corners and shiny, gleaming work surfaces. There wasn't even an open fire to toast crumpets on. Instead, it had one of those electric fires with pretend logs that glowed red with the flick of a switch.

[…]

But it didn't mean she had to stay inside, especially on an evening like this – when the setting sun was streaking the sky with shades of gold and the breeze whispered through the trees like magic.

15   'It's beautiful,' she said out loud.

That was another thing that had remained with her from the Arctic. The habit of speaking out loud to herself. April didn't consider it strange. Not until others started giving her funny looks.

Thankfully it was a Friday, which meant school was over for the week and she could do exactly as she wanted. She'd only been there a handful of months but still hadn't shaken off the feeling

20   of being the odd one out.

It didn't help that after her presentation about the plight of the polar bears – the one that had taken *ages* to prepare – most of the class had just yawned. When April had tried to wake them

up with her best roar (one she was very proud of) and then demonstrated how she could smell peanut butter from over one mile away, all they'd done was laugh and then make bear noises
25 at her from the back of the class. To make matters even more embarrassing, the teacher had pulled her aside and suggested that perhaps animal impersonations were best kept out of the classroom.

April had tried to explain in her best and most polite voice that it *wasn't* an impersonation. That she was trying to inform everyone about the problems in the Arctic – just like Lisé from
30 the Polar Institute had encouraged her. But her words were wasted. From that moment on, she was known as 'Bear Girl' and, judging from the accompanying sniggers, she wasn't sure it was a compliment.

The article in the local press hadn't helped either. Somehow a local reporter had got wind of April and her father's trip to the Arctic and since it was a slow news week, he'd wanted to tell
35 their story. Dad had been reluctant. But not April. She had seized the opportunity because surely here was a chance to tell everyone about how much the polar bears needed their help. Here was a chance to warn people how quickly the Arctic was melting! But then the article had got lots of facts wrong, including April's own name. As if she were anything like an Alice! And worst of all, rather than saying that *she* had saved Bear, the article implied that the captain of
40 the ship had done all the hard work.

April wasn't looking for brownie points or gold stars or even compliments. All she wanted was for someone to take her seriously. Especially now time was ticking for the planet.

(1) Where had April and her father been living before they moved to Stirling Road?

A   Granny Apples   B   The Antarctic   C   Number Thirty-Four

D   Bear Island   E   The city

(2) What did April find hard to accept about her new life?

A   The rudeness of the people hustling around the city

B   The gloominess of living in number Thirty-Four, Stirling Road

C   The noise and smell of the traffic and the number of people

D   The setting sun which streaked the sky with shades of gold

E   The fact that no one listened when she spoke out loud to herself

(3) Where did April toast crumpets when she lived on Bear Island?

A   On an open fire   B   In the toaster   C   Under the grill

D   On an electric fire   E   In the oven

(4) Why did others give April funny looks?

A   She spoke a strange language.

B   She could smell peanut butter from over one mile away.

C   The teacher had pulled her aside to talk to her.

D   She liked to talk out loud to herself.

E   She liked to sit outside and watch the setting sun.

Questions continue on next page

5 Why did most of the class yawn after April's presentation?

    A   They were sleepy.

    B   They were bored.

    C   To pretend they were listening.

    D   They were pretending to be bears.

    E   To show they weren't listening.

6 What had Lisé encouraged April to do?

    A   To demonstrate how bears can smell peanut butter

    B   To do animal impersonations

    C   To live by the seaside

    D   To live in a cabin on Bear Island

    E   To tell people about the plight of the Arctic

7 Why did a local reporter decide to tell April's story?

    A   He was really interested in polar bears.

    B   To raise awareness of the plight of polar bears

    C   To warn people about how quickly the Arctic was melting

    D   There wasn't much other news that week.

    E   April's dad had approached him to tell their story.

8 What interesting fact do we learn about April at the end of the extract?

    A   That she had saved a polar bear called Bear

    B   That she had been a captain of a ship

    C   That she didn't want to be taken seriously

    D   That her real name was Alice

    E   That she had got a lot of facts wrong in the article

9 '…people everywhere. Hustling, bustling and jostling every crowded minute of the day.' (line 4)

Which word is closest in meaning to 'jostling'?

    A   Juggling   **B**   Rushing   **C**   Shouting

    D   Pushing   **E**   Complaining

10 '…the breeze whispered through the trees like magic.' (line 14)

Which **two** literary techniques are used here?

    A   Alliteration and simile

    B   Personification and simile

    C   Simile and metaphor

    D   Alliteration and metaphor

    E   Personification and onomatopoeia

Score: .... / 10

Spelling

You have **6 minutes** to complete this test.

You have **12 questions** to complete within the time given.

In each question, circle the letter below the group of words containing a spelling mistake.

If there is no mistake, circle the letter **N**.

EXAMPLE

Jack used a cleer varnish to protect and strengthen the boat's teak deck.

  Ⓐ   B   C   D   **N**

---

① Mum, who is very environmentally conscious, only takes her car when it's

        A   B   C

absolutely essencial.

        D   **N**

② The form clearly stated that I should only fill in the sections that were applicible to me.

        A   B   C   D   **N**

③ The Premier League player has transfered to another club, much to the

        A   B   C

disappointment of his loyal fans.

        D   **N**

④ The scout leader lead the children to the mountain summit from where

        A   B   C

they had a magnificent view.

        D   **N**

⑤ Through the dense fog, Darius could just about perceive the chimneys

        A   B   C

of the town's industrial area.

        D   **N**

6 The steak was well presented but after one mouthful, Joe declared

    A   B   C

it to be tuff and overcooked.

    D

N

7 "It's unbelievable to think you've not watched my favourite programm!"

    A   B   C

exclaimed a shocked Debbie.

    D

N

8 After years of living a solitary existence in the Amazon rainforest,

    A   B   C

the fugitive was unreconisable.

    D

N

9 Our local comunity has started a campaign against the proposed new

    A   B   C

road through the woods.

    D

N

10 Fred is desparate to prove that he has made excellent progress

    A   B   C

in both science and geography.

    D

N

11 From the size of the crowds, it was apparant that the celebrity was

    A   B   C

revered by numerous people.

    D

N

12 The caretaker, who's shed was vandalised last night, has reported the incident to the police.

    A   B   C   D

N

Score: .... / 12

Punctuation

You have 6 minutes to complete this test.

You have 12 questions to complete within the time given.

In each question, circle the letter below the group of words containing a punctuation mistake.

If there is no mistake, circle the letter **N**.

EXAMPLE

Brogan's little brother, who's called Joe scratched his best friend's new bike in the park today.

    A   Ⓑ   C   D   N

① Faisal's new scarf which he received for his birthday, matches his hat and gloves.

    A   B   C   D   N

② I can't believe my eyes Carla has actually won the school cross-country race!

    A   B   C   D   N

③ "Finally!" Said Nikki. "I've been waiting for this delayed train for over two hours!"

    A   B   C   D   N

④ Walter had been looking forward to the easter holidays until the flight was cancelled.

    A   B   C   D   N

⑤ We always order pizza to eat when we're watching the ladies tennis final.

    A   B   C   D   N

Questions continue on next page

6 Levi has just joined an art class with her mum and her sixty-five-year-old grandmother.

     A   B   C   D   **N**

7 To celebrate his birthday Lucas decided he'd ask some friends to go abseiling with him.

     A   B   C   D   **N**

8 The hospital afternoon visiting hours (though they tend to run over

     A   B   C

are from two to three o'clock.

     D   **N**

9 Our hotel has offered an early check in time so we won't need to carry our bags around.

     A   B   C   D   **N**

10 The ambulance could only mean one thing the car accident was serious.

     A   B   C   D   **N**

11 Mum and Dad love watching childrens' films; they even know the words to most of them.

     A   B   C   D   **N**

12 The first sip of cough medicine wasn't too bad but then it got

     A   B   C

harder, and harder to swallow.

     D   **N**

Score: .... / 12

Sentence Completion

In each question, circle the letter below the word or group of words that most accurately completes each sentence.

EXAMPLE

We decided to | parting | taken | participation | participate | part take | in the Spelling Bee.
　　　　　　　　　 A 　　　 **B** 　　　 **C** 　　　　　 **(D)** 　　　　 **E**

---

① Bethan and Bill | do | done | did | finish | will finish | their homework late last night.
　　　　　　　　　　 A 　 **B** 　 **C** 　 **D** 　　 **E**

② The | sharks' | sharks | shark | shark's | shark is | been tagged to monitor its position.
　　　　 A 　　 **B** 　　 **C** 　　 **D** 　　 **E**

③ Can I please swap my book | against | in | before | beside | with | one of yours?
　　　　　　　　　　　　　　　 A 　 **B** 　 **C** 　　 **D** 　　 **E**

④ The notorious criminal escaped | being capture | capture | was captured |
　　　　　　　　　　　　　　　　　 A 　　　　　 **B** 　　　 **C**

| was capturing | capturing | for many years.
　　 D 　　　　 **E**

⑤ Ursula | pulled | will pull | pulling | pull | was pulling | two muscles during the long
　　　　 A 　　 **B** 　　 **C** 　 **D** 　　 **E**

mountain climb yesterday.

⑥ Henry's enthusiasm for football took my mind | of | for | with | about | off | the
　　　　　　　　　　　　　　　　　　　　　　 A 　 **B** 　 **C** 　 **D** 　 **E**

appalling weather.

Questions continue on next page

(7) | Have failing | Failure | Having failed | Had failed | Having fail | yet another
      A   B   C   D   E

maths test, Magda was feeling rather fed up.

(8) We wondered if we | shall | should | might | ought | better | to offer to help our
                         A   B   C   D   E

elderly neighbour in her garden.

(9) Sylvia is the | more precocious | precocious | precociousest |
                    A   B   C

| very precocious | most precocious | child I've ever met.
   D   E

(10) "Please may I | borrow | lend | loan | have a borrow of | have a loan from |
                     A   B   C   D   E

your bike?" Jenni asked Ahmed.

(11) The hikers soon realised they | should never of | should have | shouldn't of |
                                     A   B   C

| should of | should | taken the left turn at the end of the path.
   D   E

(12) Van heard the crunch of the car wheels on the gravel and | new | knowed | knowing |
                                                                A   B   C

| knowledge | knew | Dad was home.
   D   E

Score: .... / 12

In each question, circle the letter below the group of words containing a spelling mistake.

If there is no mistake, circle the letter **N**.

EXAMPLE

Jack used a cleer varnish to protect and strengthen the boat's teak deck.

(A)   B   C   D   N

---

1. The office administrator orders more stationary before the start of each new school year.

   A   B   C   D   N

2. The thistel is the flower of Scotland and one of its most recognisable symbols.

   A   B   C   D   N

3. The bruise that Adam received from his opponent was barely noticable after a few days.

   A   B   C   D   N

4. My little cousin is eager to be more independant but she is trying to run

   A   B   C

   before she can even walk!

   D   N

5. The rumours of an engagement between two of our teachers turned out to be fictitous.

   A   B   C   D   N

Questions continue on next page

6 The tree's highest bows shuddered violently in the gale, threatening

             A   **B**   **C**

to snap at any moment.

        D   **N**

7 Rachel's mood is very changable: one minute she's giggling and the next she's in a huff.

             A   **B**   **C**   **D**   **N**

8 The letter, which was marked 'private and confidencial', lay ominously on

             A   **B**   **C**

the polished bureau.

        D   **N**

9 Ushma's patterned scarf, which she received from Joe, complimented

             A   **B**   **C**

her beige waterproof coat.

        D   **N**

10 At Halloween, Stella has a preference for marshmallows toasted on the

             A   **B**   **C**

fire rather than toffee apples.

        D   **N**

11 If you are caught driving a vehicel without tax or insurance, your

             A   **B**   **C**

licence could be suspended.

        D   **N**

12 The garden centre offers a range of outdoor furniture and a massive

             A   **B**   **C**

variaty of flowers and plants.

        D   **N**

Score: .... / 12

Answers

Test 1 Comprehension

Q1   **B**   *It is clean and safe.*

'Unlike the toxic sludge of the Five Bridges river, whose length spanned the island, or the wreckage-infested ocean that surrounded it, the lagoon itself was clean, safe…'

Q2   **D**   *Quake Quarter bakery*

'…the lagoon was Minnie's second favourite place. (The bakery in Quake Quarter was the first,'

Q3   **E**   *No one could escape the high temperatures.*

'The sun showed no mercy' means there was no relief from its high temperatures.

Q4   **C**   *The islanders were getting ready for a feast.*

It is inferred in the sentences: 'They were too busy getting ready. Despite the heat and the sun, the lagoon's dark waters lay almost empty.'

Q5   **A**   *Her parents didn't believe in it.*

'…Minnie had nothing like that planned at all. Her parents didn't believe in any of that stuff on ceremony days,'

Q6   **D**   *On account of her dirty hair and large nose*

It is inferred in the sentences: '…some people privately thought was a bit too big for her face. When it was school photo time, Minnie Wadlow was always asked to stand at the back.'

Q7   **B**   *They were too polite.*

'They never said that to her face though, because they had manners.'

Q8   **D**   *Poisonous*

Q9   **D**   *Simile*

A simile describes a person or thing as being similar to someone or something else. Here, there are three similes: 'as free as a screecher bird, as smelly as a jackal cage, and as grubby as the river path.'

Q10   **A**   *heard*

Test 2 Spelling

Q1   **C**   *lightning*

Q2   **B**   *insufficient*

Q3   **A**   *temperatures*

Q4   **D**   *thoroughly*

Q5   **A**   *exaggerates*

Q6   **B**   *yacht*

Q7   **N**

Q8   **D**   *accommodation*

Q9   **B**   *mischievous*

Q10   **C**   *forty*

Q11   **D**   *languages*

Q12   **B**   *leisure*

Test 3 Punctuation

Q1   **A**   *so-called*

Q2   **C**   *Amazon*

Q3   **B**   *thought,*

Q4   **C**   *three o'clock,"*

Q5   **N**

Q6   **A**   *Museum*

Q7   **D**   *Mum's*

Q8   **B**   *hoax – was*

Q9   **C**   *later?"*

Q10   **D**   *Hill's*

Q11   **B**   *your*

Q12   **B**   *re-cover*

Test 4 Sentence Completion

Q1   **C**   *asked*

Q2   **C**   *her*

Q3   **E**   *tightly*

Q4   **A**   *ought to*

Q5   **B**   *exercising*

Q6   **B**   *filled*

Q7   **C**   *As*

Q8   **B**   *their*

Q9   **E**   *breathlessly*

Q10   **C**   *had expected*

Q11   **C**   *might be*

Q12   **C**   *lose*

Test 5 Comprehension

Q1   **B**

Paul says of the fear: 'Headlines like "Man-eating sea monster stalks the coastline killing surfer" certainly don't help.' And it '…could also be James Bond's fault as tanks full of ravenous sharks are used by the bad guys in four – yes, four – of the franchise's films).'

Q2   **D**

The writer says that although some people are attacked by sharks, 'the truth is that far more people drown in their own bathtubs than are attacked by sharks.'

Q3   **E**

Every attempt at containing the creatures in captivity failed and the animals 'perished'.

Q4   **A**

'…some things worried me more than being eaten alive, like impressing my dad. My pride was stronger than my fear…'

Test 5 answers continue on next page

Q5 *D*

A rhetorical question is asked in order to create a dramatic effect or to make a point rather than to get an answer.

Q6 *C*

'…many of the stories that we create for ourselves are horrors.' Paul means that having a fear or horror of attack, i.e. an overactive imagination, might have meant our ancestors kept away from sabre-tooth tigers.

Q7 *B*

A compound adjective is a combination of two or more words which can perform the role of an adjective in a sentence.

Q8 *A*

'realm' can mean kingdom, region, area or country.

Q9 *E*

Paul says, 'A lot of people I meet around the world tell me that they'd love to visit my home country, but they're too scared of the wildlife. Believe it or not, most Australians don't ever encounter these creatures in their entire lifetime.'

Q10 *C*

It stresses that there are as many as four James Bond films where tanks full of sharks are used by the bad guys, which could account for the terror we feel.

Test 6 Spelling

Q1	*A*	neighbour
Q2	*C*	correspond
Q3	*C*	excellent
Q4	*N*	
Q5	*B*	committee
Q6	*D*	cemetery
Q7	*B*	opportunity
Q8	*D*	occupy
Q9	*D*	muscle
Q10	*A*	attached
Q11	*C*	persuaded
Q12	*B*	rhyming

Test 7 Punctuation

Q1	*D*	Kahn.
Q2	*A*	don't
Q3	*B*	wheelbarrows
Q4	*C*	Australia; OR Australia –
Q5	*C*	sale; OR sale –
Q6	*D*	its
Q7	*C*	seventy-two
Q8	*B*	Potter
Q9	*B*	washing,"

Q10 *N*

Q11 *B* up-to-date

Q12 *D* cake and

Test 8 Sentence Completion

Q1	*B*	almost
Q2	*C*	waiting
Q3	*A*	Finally
Q4	*E*	time
Q5	*D*	numbers
Q6	*C*	mistaken
Q7	*B*	would have
Q8	*E*	did
Q9	*A*	borrow
Q10	*C*	cleverest
Q11	*C*	fault
Q12	*E*	pride

Test 9 Comprehension

Q1 *D*

'…every now and then fate deals someone a cruel blow. It dealt Dimanche Diller several, and the first and the worst of them was the loss of her mother and father.'

Q2 *A*

'Dimanche's mother was nothing if not thorough, and it was her thoroughness, even in the face of mortal danger, that saved her baby daughter's life.'

Q3 *B*

'…a monster of a wave… hung for a moment like a cliff of glass, and crashed on to the deck.'

Q4 *B*

'…they were parents themselves, and they could imagine all too well the frightful misery of this child's mother and father, if they were still alive.'

Q5 *D*

'…the wreckage of the Hippolytus had been discovered, washed up on the coast of Milos.'

Q6 *C*

Alliteration is where two or more words close together begin with the same letter or sound, in this case the 'st' sound. A simile describes a person or thing as being similar to someone or something else, here the wave is 'as strong as steel'.

Q7 *E*

'…let me tell you right now…' 'You must just take it from me…' 'If you are wondering…'

Q8 *B*

'Tearing off his jumper, he wrapped the baby in it…'

Q9 *C*

Cargo can mean goods or contents.

Q10 *A*

Personification is when human characteristics are attributed to an inanimate thing or abstract idea. Here, the wave which tore Dimanche from her mother.

Test 10 Spelling

Q1	*C*	*criticising*
Q2	*A*	*achieved*
Q3	*C*	*hindrance*
Q4	*A*	*Ancient*
Q5	*A*	*secretary*
Q6	*D*	*century*
Q7	*B*	*equipped*
Q8	*D*	*average*
Q9	*A*	*unexpected*
Q10	*B*	*occurred*
Q11	*B*	*government's*
Q12	*N*	

Test 11 Punctuation

Q1	*A*	*eaten,*
Q2	*C*	*following:*
Q3	*C*	*raining –*
Q4	*B*	*who's*
Q5	*N*	
Q6	*D*	*her).*
Q7	*B*	*Wales and*
Q8	*D*	*mistake –* OR *mistake. What*
Q9	*A*	*increased,*
Q10	*B*	*hats,*
Q11	*D*	*last few*
Q12	*D*	*Jim 'The King' Flynn*

Test 12 Sentence Completion

Q1	*C*	*than*
Q2	*C*	*had run*
Q3	*E*	*would*
Q4	*B*	*feet*
Q5	*E*	*children's*
Q6	*B*	*who's*
Q7	*D*	*brought*
Q8	*A*	*Against*
Q9	*B*	*satisfying*
Q10	*D*	*In*
Q11	*C*	*lit*
Q12	*E*	*having eaten*

Test 13 Comprehension

Q1 *B*

The description of his clothes implies he has good fashion sense and is wealthy. He is wearing a French hat so he had money to buy a hat from abroad: French fashion was/is held in high esteem. The velvet coat, the shiny sword, the lace at his chin, no wrinkles in his trousers and full-length boots all indicate money and a sense of fashion.

Q2 *C*

We know he's expecting Bess by his request for a kiss. By a process of elimination, we know it can't be any of the others.

Q3 *A*

He is a highwayman which means he is a criminal. His prize will be the theft of gold.

Q4 *A*

If you stand to attention, you stand bolt upright. The soldiers tied Bess up so she was upright and able to see the highwayman's approach, but also he would be able to see her which is what the soldiers want – she is the bait.

Q5 *B*

In the last verse we learn: 'Not till the dawn he heard it'

Q6 *E*

Onomatopoeia is the use or creation of a word that sounds like the noise it describes. Here, the poet has created the word 'tlot-tlot' which sounds like the horse's hooves.

Q7 *D*

She managed to fire the musket (gun). Earlier, we learn that 'the trigger at least was hers!', meaning that her finger had found the trigger.

Q8 *B*

To strive is to struggle.

Q9 *E*

The poem is a romantic ballad, which tells a story (narrative) of love and loss.

Q10 *D*

A metaphor describes something by referring to something else which is the same in a particular way. For example, 'the road was a ribbon of moonlight' meaning that the road was like a ribbon of moonlight.

Test 14 Spelling

Q1	*D*	*inconvenient*
Q2	*A*	*harassed*
Q3	*B*	*conscious*
Q4	*A*	*bruised*
Q5	*C*	*bargained*
Q6	*B*	*dictionary*
Q7	*N*	

Test 14 answers continue on next page

Q8	D	categories
Q9	A	awkward
Q10	B	nuisance
Q11	C	guaranteed
Q12	A	twelfths

Test 15 Punctuation

Q1	D	sped off
Q2	A	At first,
Q3	B	Dad.
Q4	A	surprise!
Q5	B	this: OR this –
Q6	D	School
Q7	D	me.
Q8	C	delighted when
Q9	N	
Q10	C	shan't
Q11	C	you? OR you!
Q12	B	me;

Test 16 Sentence Completion

Q1	A	were rung
Q2	E	lightning
Q3	B	which
Q4	C	meddle
Q5	D	was lying
Q6	A	you know
Q7	D	all right
Q8	B	accept
Q9	E	emigrating
Q10	C	proceeded
Q11	A	reference
Q12	B	ascent

Test 17 Comprehension

Q1 B

'the sheer agony of panting up steep slopes in the summer sun, the sharp smell of my father's sweat… Then the gritty feel of the granite under your fingers…'

Q2 C

'double-edge pleasure' means that on the one hand he got a lot of pleasure from climbing, but on the other hand it was upsetting because his brother was killed while climbing.

Q3 C

He was 'the paragon of climbers' is used to describe Mallory, not Uncle Hunch.

Q4 D

Uncle Hunch pressed his chest, which released the blockage.

Q5 E

General C. G. Bruce was the expedition leader.

Q6 A

Alliteration is where two or more words close together begin with the same letter or sound, in this case the 's' sound.

Q7 D

He is: talented – double first degree, gifted artist and musician; determined – joined the Everest expedition and had a long-standing record for going the highest without oxygen; strong – Bruce described Uncle Hunch's 'strength on the mountain'.

Q8 A

If Mallory had made it to the top, he might have taken some photographs which would prove he got there.

Q9 B

A simile describes a person or thing as being similar to someone or something else, here 'like a polished steel floor'.

Q10 A

'foremost' can mean leading, first, top, or first in time or rank.

Test 18 Spelling

Q1	B	amateur
Q2	N	
Q3	B	sacrifices
Q4	D	rhythm
Q5	C	symbol
Q6	B	competitive
Q7	C	pronunciation
Q8	D	queue
Q9	A	Parliament
Q10	D	system
Q11	A	embarrassed
Q12	D	prejudice

Test 19 Punctuation

Q1	A	men's
Q2	D	pens
Q3	N	
Q4	A	they're
Q5	B	key,
Q6	B	school
Q7	C	bedtime; his OR bedtime – his
Q8	B	Jess' OR Jess's
Q9	D	summer
Q10	A	Monty?"
Q11	C	councillor, then
Q12	C	know," OR know!"

Test 20 Sentence Completion

Q1 **C** *where*
Q2 **D** *asked*
Q3 **B** *led*
Q4 **E** *thorough*
Q5 **A** *Whom*
Q6 **B** *passed*
Q7 **D** *besides*
Q8 **B** *hadn't taken*
Q9 **C** *theirs*
Q10 **A** *council*
Q11 **C** *of*
Q12 **E** *we're going*

Test 21 Comprehension

Q1 **B**

The guide says, 'It's never taken me more than five minutes to find turtles' so he is teasing them, making them think it could be a while.

Q2 **A**

'…archaeological sites dating from as early as 840 BC to the arrival of Columbus in 1493.' From 840 BC to 1493 is over two thousand years.

Q3 **E**

Snorkelling in Scott Beach Bay is 'the main event' for James.

Q4 **D**

After 20 minutes, they haven't seen any turtles but he is also red from the 'blazing sunshine'.

Q5 **C**

The remora uses its sucker to ride on top of the turtle's shell, feeding on its scraps and faeces, and sharing its protective shell.

Q6 **E**

'The water is thick with turtles…'

Q7 **A**

The turtle defecates. James is swimming behind her when suddenly she releases 'her own soup'. He describes it as 'abhorrent' which means it is foul. Bouillabaisse is a rich stew or soup of fish and vegetables.

Q8 **D**

According to general belief

Q9 **B**

'The water is as warm as the toddlers' pool at your local swimming baths,'

Q10 **D**

A metaphor describes something by referring to something else which is the same in a particular way. Here, James is saying that in following the turtle and the remora fish, they are like a zen procession. 'Zen' is a form of the Buddhist religion that focuses on meditation.

Test 22 Spelling

Q1 **B** *foreign*
Q2 **N**
Q3 **B** *sincere*
Q4 **C** *existence*
Q5 **B** *developed*
Q6 **B** *familiar*
Q7 **C** *available*
Q8 **C** *profession*
Q9 **A** *principal*
Q10 **C** *interfere*
Q11 **B** *borough*
Q12 **B** *solemn*

Test 23 Punctuation

Q1 **C** *friends:*
Q2 **A** *truck's*
Q3 **A** *Shamelessly,*
Q4 **B** *tournament;* OR *tournament –*
Q5 **C** *teachers'*
Q6 **N**
Q7 **C** *party,"*
Q8 **A** *Day*
Q9 **B** *Jamal's*
Q10 **B** *she'll*
Q11 **B** *years,*
Q12 **D** *Crunch*

Test 24 Sentence Completion

Q1 **E** *in*
Q2 **D** *because*
Q3 **B** *which*
Q4 **E** *dogs*
Q5 **A** *courtiers*
Q6 **C** *favours*
Q7 **B** *It's*
Q8 **A** *shook*
Q9 **E** *even though*
Q10 **C** *bought*
Q11 **D** *dog's*
Q12 **C** *safely*

Test 25 Comprehension

Q1   **E**

'…they had sold their tall and gloomy city house…'

Q2   **C**

'The constant noise and smog of cars and motorbikes, with their never-ending stench of exhaust, had been the most horrible shock. And people. So many people everywhere. Hustling, bustling and jostling every crowded minute of the day.'

Q3   **A**

It is implied in the sentence: 'There wasn't even an open fire to toast crumpets on.' which suggests she used to do it.

Q4   **D**

'The habit of speaking out loud to herself. April didn't consider it strange. Not until others started giving her funny looks.'

Q5   **B**

'It didn't help that after her presentation about the plight of the polar bears – the one that had taken ages to prepare – most of the class had just yawned.'

Q6   **E**

'…she was trying to inform everyone about the problems in the Arctic – just like Lisé from the Polar Institute had encouraged her.'

Q7   **D**

'…since it was a slow news week, he'd wanted to tell their story.'

Q8   **A**

'…rather than saying that she had saved Bear, the article implied that the captain of the ship had done all the hard work.'

Q9   **D**

Pushing

Q10   **B**

Personification is when human characteristics are attributed to an inanimate thing or abstract idea. Here, 'the breeze whispered'. A simile describes a person or thing as being similar to someone or something else. Here, the whispering breeze is 'like magic'.

Test 26 Spelling

Q1   **D**   essential

Q2   **D**   applicable

Q3   **B**   transferred

Q4   **A**   led

Q5   **N**

Q6   **D**   tough

Q7   **C**   programme

Q8   **D**   unrecognisable

Q9   **A**   community

Q10   **A**   desperate

Q11   **B**   apparent

Q12   **A**   whose

Test 27 Punctuation

Q1   **A**   scarf,

Q2   **B**   eyes – OR eyes: OR eyes! OR eyes.

Q3   **A**   said

Q4   **C**   Easter

Q5   **D**   ladies'

Q6   **N**

Q7   **B**   birthday,

Q8   **C**   over)

Q9   **B**   check-in

Q10   **C**   thing: the OR thing – the

Q11   **B**   children's

Q12   **D**   harder and

Test 28 Sentence Completion

Q1   **C**   did

Q2   **D**   shark's

Q3   **E**   with

Q4   **B**   capture

Q5   **A**   pulled

Q6   **E**   off

Q7   **C**   Having failed

Q8   **D**   ought

Q9   **E**   most precocious

Q10   **A**   borrow

Q11   **B**   should have

Q12   **E**   knew

Test 29 Spelling

Q1   **B**   stationery

Q2   **A**   thistle

Q3   **D**   noticeable

Q4   **B**   independent

Q5   **D**   fictitious

Q6   **A**   boughs

Q7   **B**   changeable

Q8   **B**   confidential

Q9   **C**   complemented

Q10   **N**

Q11   **B**   vehicle

Q12   **D**   variety